Extraordinary Seaman

THE MACMILLAN COMPANY
NEW YORK • CHICAGO
DALLAS • ATLANTA • SAN FRANCISCO
LONDON • MANILA

BRETT-MACMILLAN LTD.
TORONTO

J. P. W. MALLALIEU

Extraordinary
Seaman

ILLUSTRATED BY

MUDGE-MARRIATT

NEW YORK

THE MACMILLAN COMPANY

1958

© J. P. W. Mallalieu 1957

First Printing

Printed in the United States of America

Library of Congress catalog card number: 58-8155

FOR
ANN AND BEN MALLALIEU

Contents

Preface

CAPTAIN COCHRANE went to sea in the Royal Navy's greatest period. He became one of the finest sea fighters Britain has ever known. His scientific ingenuity and imaginative genius made him a pioneer of combat methods which were only fully developed nearly one hundred and fifty years later in the second world war. By his skill and daring he did more than any one individual to bring independence to three great countries, which, together, are larger than the whole United States.

Yet today his name is almost unknown even in the British Isles. For every ten thousand Britons who have heard of Davy Crockett—a minor American frontiersman during one of the less creditable periods in United States history— perhaps one has heard of Captain Lord Cochrane, tenth Earl of Dundonald.

We have a long history from which to choose our heroes. We prefer doing to talking. Our national arrogance lies in under- rather than over-statement.

But I think that our ignorance of Cochrane is odd even for us.

This book tells a little of him, but by no means all.

J. P. W. Mallalieu

ICKFORD, 1957

1. Men from the North

SCANDINAVIAN SEAFARERS drove their steep prows through the mists of the North Sea. They leaped through surf and spray on to the rocky beaches of Scotland and fought their way inland. They killed those who opposed them, murdered those who did not, took away what they could carry and burned what they had to leave. They were the finest and fiercest seamen of their age.

Some of them in time settled in the country they had begun by ravaging; one founded the family of Coveran, or Cochrane, and, in so doing, he helped to shape the future history of the world. His descendants were already well known in the thirteenth century, and by the fifteenth one of them, Robert, had become the chief adviser to King James III. He was not born a courtier. Indeed, he assigned such lands as he had to his son and began to study architecture. But the King happened to see him fight a duel and was so impressed by his strength that he brought him to Court.

Robert Cochrane, besides being strong, was competent. He became the King's right hand, to the annoyance of the

Scottish nobles, who thought him no better than a tradesman, and called him the 'mason chiel'.

So far from being upset by the opposition of the established hierarchy, Cochrane flouted it. He wore extravagant clothes, spent money lavishly, and lost no chance of expressing contempt for people who were born into high positions without having earned them by ability and hard work.

The established nobility took Cochrane's elevation to the Earldom of Mar as the crowning insult. A commoner who in those days became the favourite of a weak king and tried to imbue him with strength to stand up to the vested interests of the nobility was bound to die before his time. When the nobles found that the chief place in the kingdom was given to such a man and that he was filling with his own type the places which hitherto had been the hereditary perquisites of noble sons, they took matters into their own hands.

A Council of State was summoned in the King's name at an Edinburgh church, and when Cochrane arrived he found the door shut against him. He knocked and was asked his name.

' 'Tis I, the Earl of Mar.'

The door was opened and he walked inside. At once he was accosted by the fiery Earl of Angus, who saw that he was preceded by an attendant carrying a golden helmet set with precious stones, that he was dressed in velvet, and that he wore an ostentatiously brilliant chain of gold around his neck.

Angus snatched at the golden chain—'A rope will become thee better,' he said.

'You have been too long a hunter of mischief,' said another noble, seizing Cochrane's golden hunting horn.

Cochrane was caught by surprise. 'My Lords,' he said, 'is it jest or earnest?'

'It is good and earnest and so thou shalt find it,' replied the nobles.

They tied his arms and jostled him to the bridge at Lauder. When he saw that he was indeed to be hanged from the bridge, he said: 'Let me at least be hanged with silken cords from my own pavilion.' The nobles took this as yet another sign of arrogance, and hanged him with the coarsest ropes they could find.

He was the first Cochrane to discover that it can be dangerous to clash with the establishment; but he was not the last.

*　　　*　　　*

During Stuart times six Cochrane sons fought on the side of Charles I and gave not only their blood but also their treasure. Subsequently, those who survived were heavily fined by Cromwell. As a result of loans to the King and fines to the Protector, many of them were ruined.

But one, Sir William Cochrane, managed not merely to maintain but to improve his position. Buchanan says of him that he was 'very carefully educated in grammar learning in his youth, whence he was removed to the university, where, having applied himself indefatigably to his studies and highly improved his natural endowments with academical learning, he removed from thence after he had taken the degree of Master of Arts, and studied our laws'.

Though he was a King's man, he was no sycophant and strongly opposed Charles's plans for interfering with the Scottish Church. Yet he became a Member of Parliament, a Privy Councillor, and, subsequently, first Earl of Dundonald.

Few Cochranes, however, could keep out of trouble. Two of Sir William's sons joined the rebellions of Argyll and Monmouth, and one of them, John, was nearly hanged, like his fifteenth-century ancestor. He was brave, undisciplined and headstrong. When his fellow rebels hesitated to enter Ayrshire, he shamed them by saying that he would go alone, armed only with a pitchfork. They were heavily defeated, and John himself was captured and sent to London. His father's good name and a bribe of £5,000 alone saved him from the gallows.

Had it not been for this timely bribe, Britain would never have known the man who eventually became one of her greatest seamen. For John, after his rescue, had a large family, and one of his descendants was the Thomas Cochrane whom Napoleon nicknamed the 'sea wolf', whom the Spaniards called 'the Devil', and whose bones today lie beside those of the Unknown Soldier in Westminster Abbey.

* * *

Thomas was born on December 14th, 1775, at Annsfield in Lanarkshire, the eldest son of the ninth Earl of Dundonald.

The ninth Earl was streaked with the stubbornness, brilliance and eccentricity which ran through the Cochrane family. He had a passion for natural science, and spent the money he inherited or acquired by marriage on innumerable experiments and innumerable and usually disastrous attempts to commercialize the results. He was the personal friend of such men as James Watt and Priestley, and was wholly absorbed in the ferment of ideas which was then developing the Industrial Revolution.

His estates, such as they were, were gradually sold to pay for his scientific pursuits, until nothing remained except the rambling Culross Abbey, which he turned into a haphazard laboratory, and some adjoining coal mines to which he clung as the source of material for his experiments.

The results of his experiments in the application of chemicals to agriculture are still being applied today. He invented methods of preserving sails, which the Admiralty adopted, and of preserving ships' bottoms, which was welcomed by those who bought ships and rejected by those who sold them. He was the first man to extract tar from coal. But one discovery that eluded him was the secret of making money.

During his tar experiments he stumbled on something which could have made him one of the richest men in the country. One day, working at the tar-kiln he had built in his grounds, he saw flames playing in the air above the coal which he was distilling. Obviously the vapours were inflammable.

With no special aim in view, he decided to canalize these vapours instead of allowing them to escape into the empty air; and the best means to hand was an old gun-barrel, which he fitted to the kiln.

As soon as the barrel was in position, he put a flame to the muzzle and a brilliantly vivid light, clearly visible for miles around, blazed out across the nearby waters of the River Forth.

The Earl was like a child with a new toy. He was still babbling about this delightful phenomenon when he next visited his friend Mr. James Watt. Mr. Watt was as intrigued as the Earl. But though the key was in the lock, neither of them turned it.

That was left to one of Mr. Watt's assistants, who overheard the talk, pondered on it and suddenly saw what it could mean. As a result, streets which hitherto had been dark, and houses which had been lit only by foul-smelling lamps or candles, began for the first time to see gaslight. The Earl shared in the general illumination, but did not receive a penny for it.

Because he was so helplessly uncommercial, he was never able to pay for the proper education of his children. For a time, while he was in funds, he did employ a French tutor. But this man was not only a Catholic, but even went so far as to shoot rooks on the Sabbath, which so enraged the elders of the kirk that he had to leave.

Thereafter for a time the children merely picked up what they could as they ran wild in the laboratory or on the ruins and moors near the Abbey. Subsequently, on the death of their mother, their father married again, and used a small portion of the dowry from his second wife to send his sons to school in London. But the greater part of the dowry, of course, flowed into his experiments, and when that was all lost the boys had to be withdrawn from their London school.

Perhaps because his chances of getting a formal education were so fleeting, the ninth Earl's eldest son Thomas worked exceptionally hard at his books. But even more important was the fact that he had inherited his father's lively and inquisitive mind, and had the chance at home, amid his father's experiments, to pick up knowledge which would have been denied him in a formal school. The habit of learning whenever and wherever he could, which he either inherited or acquired in childhood, remained with him for the rest of his life.

Though the father was feckless about his own affairs and about the formal education of his children, he was traditionally dictatorial in deciding what careers his children should adopt. He was determined that Thomas should go into the

6

Army, and, after the custom of those days, got him a commission in the Horse Guards when he was still a young boy.

As training for this career, Thomas was put in the charge of a tough old sergeant. Worse, he was forced to wear a uniform of his father's own design. He himself wrote years later:

'My hair, cherished with boyish pride, was formally cut and plastered back with a vile composition of candle-grease and flour. . . . My neck, from childhood open to the Lowland breeze, was encased in an inflexible leathern collar or stock, selected according to my preceptor's notions of military propriety, thus almost verging on strangulation. A blue semi-military tunic with red collar and cuffs in imitation of the Windsor uniform was provided, and to complete the tout ensemble, my father, who was a determined Whig partisan, insisted on my wearing yellow waistcoat and breeches, yellow being the Whig colour of which I was admonished never to be ashamed.'

The misery which this uniform caused to a small boy who hitherto had dressed and done much as he pleased was increased by the sneers of other boys whom he met in the streets. After one brush with a gang of youths at Charing Cross, Thomas ran home in tears and begged his father to excuse him from joining the Army. His father beat him smartly and told him to do as he was told. That, however, was one lesson which throughout his life Thomas was not wholly able to learn.

*   *   *

Almost since he could remember, he had wanted to join the Navy. Many of his relatives were naval men. His uncle, Alexander, was already a captain. His maternal grandfather, Captain Gilchrist, had fought a gallant action in 1758, when,

7

commanding a ship of only thirty-two guns, he had taken the French forty-gun ship *Danae*, killing eighty-two of the enemy's crew for the loss of only one of his own. His own father, too, had actually served in the Navy for a short time, but had found one cruise enough, and was determined that his son should not enter a service which he himself had found so distasteful.

But what was in the boy's blood could not be put out. As a very small child he had surreptitiously taken the sheets from his bed and used them as sails for a small boat in the Firth of Forth; and from the time when he was conscious of anything, he had been conscious of the belief that his future lay on the sea.

Eventually his determination wore down even the determination of his father. It was agreed that Thomas should join his uncle's ship. Of course there was no money to pay for his kit; but the Earl of Hopetoun, a friend of the family, advanced him £100, and, with his father's gold watch—the only patrimony he was ever to receive—he left home. On June 27th, 1793, at the age of seventeen and a half, he eagerly followed his uncle up the gangway to step for the first time on the deck of a British man-of-war.

*　　*　　*

Jack Larmour, the first lieutenant of the *Hind*, lying at Sheerness, was at the gangway as his captain came aboard. He was suitably deferential. But he was also watchful.

Larmour had begun his naval life as an ordinary seaman. By hard work, unadorned by social graces and unaided by social influence, he had at last, most unusually, been commissioned. His whole world was bounded by the taffrail and the bowsprit. He had mastered the technical details of his

8

profession with his hands rather than with his head. He was educated by experience alone. Even if he had known what theory was, he would have distrusted it; and he did know what patronage was—he had seen young fops and ne'er-do-wells placed above his head into positions which they could not maintain except on his shoulders. He distrusted and resented this; and here, behind his captain, was another lanky specimen of patronage, eager-eyed no doubt, but sure, all the same, to be dead weight.

The first lieutenant listened to his captain with an impatience which he managed somehow to conceal. He even glanced without open hostility at the youth who stood by his captain's side. He would deal with him later. This whipper-snapper—he was the captain's nephew, wasn't he? And wasn't he a Lord? Hadn't he held a commission in the Army? If so, what was he doing aboard the *Hind*?

'Kicked out of the Army, I shouldn't wonder,' said Larmour to himself, 'and now his family has dropped him into my lap as though I were a swiving cushion. I'll give him cushions!'

Lieutenant Larmour looked casually at the masthead.

Meanwhile, as his uncle chatted easily and the first lieutenant tried to reply with something more than grunts, young Cochrane looked with interest but with some puzzlement at Larmour.

Had he heard right? Was this man really the *Hind*'s first lieutenant? Larmour was wearing 'square rig', or seaman's dress. A marlinspike was strung round his neck. A lump of grease was in his hand. He had climbed down from the rigging to greet his visitors and was now having obvious difficulty with the civilities.

While the captain chatted, the eyes of the first lieutenant

9

strayed back to the rigging, where there was work to be done. Perhaps the captain himself became aware of the tenseness, and with a 'Well, I must be off, my boy,' to Cochrane, and an unnecessary 'Lick him into shape!' to Larmour, he went ashore, leaving the shiny midshipman and the case-hardened seaman alone.

'Get your traps below,' said Larmour, and turned back to the rigging.

Cochrane carried his immediate belongings to the midshipmen's berth, and was beginning to unpack when uproar broke out above his head.

'Is this *Lord* Cochrane's chest?' roared a voice, putting such feeling into the word 'Lord' that Cochrane wished he had never heard of such a title. 'Does *Lord* Cochrane think he is going to bring a cabin aboard too? The swiving service is going to the swiving devil. Get the swiving thing up to the swiving main deck.'

There was a sound of heaving, of heavy feet, of expletives bursting from Larmour's half-open lips, of a crash as the chest was dumped on the main deck. Then, for a moment, there was silence, and Cochrane, blushing to himself, turned again to his unpacking. Almost at once he was interrupted by a seaman.

'May I have the keys for your chest, sir? For the first lieutenant, sir.'

This seemed strange. But the noise that followed, though familiar, was stranger still. It was the sound of a saw. Jack Larmour had emptied the chest and was now cutting it in half to make sure it would fit into the space for midshipman's baggage.

'Why do swiving midshipmen have swiving chests like this? And why do we have swiving midshipmen?' he shouted.

'And why do these swiving landlubbers have to put the swiving keyhole in the swiving middle where no one can get at the swiver? Why the swiving hell don't they put the swiver at the swiving end?'

Cochrane looked at the now ruined chest, to which so much of his £100 loan had gone, gravely thanked the first lieutenant, and retired again below.

Inevitably a contest developed between the two. Young Cochrane was not going to be punished by Jack Larmour. He would learn everything he could and even do everything he was told. But Jack said, 'I've never heard of such a thing as a faultless swiving midshipman,' and waited his time. He did see, though, that Cochrane was not the idle young fop he had expected, and acknowledged this, typically, by reserving for him all his strongest language.

'I never swear at waisters,' he said. 'That's only spending swiving wind for nothing.'

There was in fact only one thing aboard the *Hind* on which Larmour was ready to waste breath. That was the ship's parrot, a bird which had distinguished itself by learning all the bo'sun's pipes by heart. Once when a lady visitor was being hoisted aboard from a boat, the parrot loudly piped 'Let go!', and the lady was dumped in the sea. Larmour would readily have wrung the parrot's neck, but it was the captain's special pet. He could therefore only rave, which merely taught the parrot bad language as well as the bo'sun's pipes.

Cochrane did his work well on his first cruise. The *Hind* was sent to watch the coast of Norway for privateers and enemy convoys. But none was found, and the young midshipman had all his time free to learn seamanship under the eye of Larmour. He slipped up only once.

After a long spell of duty in the cold, he went below for a quick hot drink. But as soon as he returned to the upper deck, he heard the dreaded words: 'Masthead, youngster!' The temperature was below zero, but despite frozen fingers Cochrane had to climb to the masthead and stay there. Larmour looked up at him from time to time, obviously calculating to a fraction just how much the young man could endure without crashing to the deck below, and just as Cochrane felt that he could hold no longer he was ordered down. He saw to it that he was never mastheaded again.

He and the first lieutenant became firm friends. When the *Hind* returned to England, his uncle was transferred to the *Thetis*, and Cochrane and Larmour were transferred with him. The *Thetis* at the time was refitting at Sheerness, and the officers were allowed to go home on leave. But instead, as soon as he heard that Larmour intended to stay aboard and help with the refitting, Cochrane asked permission to stay with him. Larmour agreed, on condition that Cochrane would get out of officer's dress and wear square rig.

So with a knife in his belt and marlinspike in his hand the midshipman was put through all the refinements of knotting, splicing and other aspects of the seaman's craft, until even Larmour was prepared to say that in another swiving twenty years he mightn't be too bad.

As a result of this tuition, Cochrane quickly passed his examinations for lieutenant, and was in time transferred to Lord Keith's flagship, the *Barfleur*, then operating in the Mediterranean. During that cruise, he had his only meeting with Lord Nelson, and, characteristically, Nelson found time to discuss naval tactics with this junior lieutenant.

'Never mind manœuvres. Always go straight at 'em,' Nelson told him. Cochrane understood what Nelson meant, and through his own career he disregarded what were then the stylized conventions of engaging an enemy. His sole concern was to get himself in a position to strike, and then to strike hard.

In the *Barfleur*, and subsequently in the *Queen Charlotte*, Cochrane saw plenty of action, but the feat which was to win him his first command was not a fight.

Lord Nelson's squadron had just captured the French ship *Généreux*, a seventy-four, and Cochrane was placed in temporary command as prize master. He was given a crew of sick and invalided men collected from the rest of the fleet, and told to take the *Généreux* into Port Mahon. Shortly after he had put to sea, a gale sprang up, and, because the rigging had not been properly set, the masts swayed with every roll. It was dangerous even for fit men to go aloft; but Cochrane persuaded his invalids to do their duty by going aloft himself. When the gale abated, he set the hands to work and put the ship into some sort of order, so that both ship and crew arrived safely at Port Mahon.

Because of this performance, and to his great delight, Cochrane was given his first command, the *Speedy*.

2. Giant-killer

AS SHE LAY AT PORT MAHON, MINORCA, in the early spring of 1800, the *Speedy* looked a miserable ship. She was a brig of 158 tons burden, designed to take a small cargo and crew along the coasts of peacetime Britain. But now she had been converted to a man-of-war.

The new captain went at once to his cabin. He could not sit, because, after allowing for the bunk and table. there was no room for a chair; and he could not stand because the deckhead was only five feet high and he himself was six feet two. He saw that if he wanted to shave he would have to push his head through the skylight and fix his shaving mirror on the deck above.

He went to look at the crew's quarters. These were far worse. They were so dark that even if the men crouched as they moved and so avoided any hazards above them, they risked cracking their heads against pillars or barking their shins against the barrels and other tackle which littered the deck at their feet. Everywhere there was the smell of damp, sweat and decayed food.

Cochrane surveyed all this—if 'surveyed' is the right word

14

for a man who has had to bend himself into a right angle and is peering through gloom. Then he went silently on deck to look at the fourteen four-pounder guns which were his only armament.

'Popguns!' he said, in his quiet Lowland voice.

Fourteen four-pounders, with a maximum range of a hundred yards! How would he fare against twelve- or eighteen-pounders firing two thousand yards or more? Surely the dockyard could do better than this?

He looked thoughtfully over the side for a few moments, and then, with an impish look in his eye, went ashore and strode purposefully away.

He came back with two dockyard officials. Together they peered at the guns, shaking their heads. After a minute or so Cochrane abruptly left them and strolled to the other side of the ship. When he returned there was a bulge in his pockets and a grin on his face.

'Do you know what I have got here?' he said, tapping the bulge. 'I have got a broadside in my pockets.' His pockets were stuffed with the metal balls which were all that his popguns could fire. He stalked up and down the quarter-deck while the dockyard officials laughed.

True, Cochrane was exceptionally strong. But even a much weaker man could easily have carried his load, for the total broadside weighed no more than a sack of potatoes. That was all right against small men-of-war or unarmed merchantmen, but Cochrane already saw himself matched against the full might of France and Spain.

The dockyard officials promised to see what they could do, and, with no more than the usual dockyard delay, two twelve-pounders were delivered to the *Speedy*.

Cochrane's men sweated through the day, putting the

guns in position, while their captain stood by with shining eyes and directed. At last the work was finished, but as the men straightened their backs they saw that their captain's eyes were shining no longer.

'We'll not be able to work those guns,' he said. 'There's not enough room.'

It looked as though he was right. The *Speedy*'s deck was so cramped that any gun's crew trying to work a twelve-pounder would tumble over itself. But Cochrane was not going to waste all that work and throw away his one chance of having an effective armament unless he was sure. He ordered the crew to load one of the guns and fire it out to sea.

The trial shoot went well. The men did get in each other's way, but that awkwardness might just be lack of practice. Perhaps they would be able to work the guns after all. Then suddenly a seaman shouted and pointed to the deck. The planking over which the gun carriage ran in recoil had split wide open. The *Speedy* was so decrepit that the concussion of one shot from a twelve-pounder had shivered her timbers.

The two new guns were returned to the dockyard.

There was now only one thing for it. If the *Speedy* could not outgun her opponents she must try to outsail them; and at the moment she could not sail at all because she had recently lost her main yard in a storm.

Cochrane looked up to where the main yard should have been and went away to think. How could he make the *Speedy* live up to her name? He would have to fit an extra-long main yard to give himself an extra spread of canvas. Of course there were risks about this. If he had got too much sail on too small a ship and ran into a storm he might capsize. Well, he considered himself seaman enough to avoid that. At any rate he was young enough to risk it. The *Speedy* should have her extra sail.

Had she any other assets at all?

Like any new captain, Cochrane began to speculate about his crew. He knew that conditions aboard ship were so foul and pay so bad—an ordinary seaman got half a crown a week, paid months, sometimes years, in arrear—that few men volunteered for the Navy. So convicted criminals who, offered a choice of gaol or the Royal Navy, chose the fate they did not know, and landsmen, able-bodied, but not apparently able-footed, who happened to be caught in sea-port streets by the press gang, made up the rest of the complement.

Cochrane, however, had great faith in Britons as seamen. Even those who had lived farthest inland could and did learn seamanship quickly, provided they were well led; and he knew that his crew had been well led by their previous commander.

He was soon to find out that, surprisingly, his crew were not even dissatisfied about pay. In addition to their regular wages, all British seamen were entitled to a share in the value of any merchantman or man-of-war which their ship captured, and as, in her recent cruises, the *Speedy* had captured more than her share of prizes, her crew were in the money.

Yes, he seemed to have a good crew. If he got that extra sail he would have a fast ship. They would be able to do not only the routine blockade control for which their Lordships intended them, but also the far more adventurous work, beyond the bounds of duty, which the young captain already had in his mind's eye.

Or would they? There was sudden activity on deck and

Cochrane climbed from his cabin to investigate. His new main yard had arrived. Strictly, it was not new and it was not a main yard. The dockyard had sent him a foretopgallant yard from a captured French ship, a minor spar for a minor ship. He looked at it with some annoyance. His annoyance increased when he looked at the dockyard instructions. Even this minor spar, it appeared, was considered too large for the insignificant *Speedy*. He was to cut it down to what the dockyard considered a suitable size.

He was thoroughly alarmed. Larger guns he knew to be impossible, But now he was forbidden to have the extra sail. However good his crew, the *Speedy* would be condemned to 'safe' routine. Then suddenly he smiled, and sent for the carpenter.

'Get your saw and take half an inch off each end of that yard,' he said.

The carpenter looked at him blankly. There had been rumours about the Cochrane family. Was the new captain a bit mad? However, there was something determined about the boyish eyes which looked at him. The carpenter scratched his head and did as he was told.

The captain had the yard hoisted into position and then ordered his crew to fix the rigging in a way that was new to them. They too scratched their heads, but did as they were told.

Cochrane then sent for dockyard officials to inspect the ship and clear him ready for sea. During the inspection he made sure that the attention of the officials was fully occupied. They had no time for more than a glance at the main yard.

'You will see,' he said, pointing to the brightness of the newly sawn ends, 'I have had the yard cut down.'

The officials looked up, saw that the wood was fresh where the carpenter had cut it, but, because of the unorthodox rigging which Cochrane had devised, they failed to realize that the yard was virtually as long as before. They cleared the *Speedy* for sea and away she went, under topsails and topgallantsails only, until she was beyond recall.

*　　*　　*

Britain at this time was at war both with France and with Spain, and the work of the Navy was not only to keep open the sea lanes to Britain herself, but also, by interception and blockade, to prevent supplies from reaching Britain's enemies.

Cochrane in his small ship was sent to harry what enemy shipping he could find off the coast of Spain. He was to have an independent command. He was to work on his own, rather like one of the many privateers which still darted about the seas of the world and pounced on whatever they could find. It was the job that Cochrane most wanted. Throughout his life he never found it easy to take orders from a superior, nor to work with others of equal rank. He was at his best when on his own; and in this job he would be on his own. For months at a time he would be many miles from a friendly port. His only way of communicating with another ship was by visual signals, and he might have to sail for weeks at a time without sighting a ship that was friendly. For most of the time he would have to rely on his own resources and his own resource.

He knew the risks that he would run. He had no doubt that he could handle any merchantman he might run across; but there was the danger that at any moment he might find himself without warning within range of enemies whose fire-power and speed were greatly superior to his own. Today a sloop cruising on her own would have radar warning of a battleship's approach, but the only warning Cochrane could expect would be the sight of towering masts coming over the horizon.

But instead of this making him cautious, Cochrane decided to adopt tactics which would actually increase the risk. Until he arrived there, the normal practice of British men-of-war who were watching the Spanish coast was to lay well off shore during the night and come in to attack in daytime. This seemed prudent, because the coast was bordered with shoals and submerged rocks, which could easily wreck a navigator who did not know the area intimately.

Unfortunately, it made things safer for the enemy coastal ships, whose captains in daylight got good warning of any British approach, and so had plenty of time to run for shelter in the nearest harbour or under the guns of the nearest fort.

Cochrane decided that this would not do. He would lay off shore well out of sight during daytime, and would attack during the night or just before dawn, when his approach would be concealed until the last moment. This gave him a better chance of making captures; but it also increased the risk not only that he might founder but also that he would come within range of an overwhelming enemy force before he could identify it.

He thought over these risks as he sailed away from Port Mahon, and began to plan the tactics which he hoped would keep him out of trouble. Some of the tricks he had in mind were commonplaces of the day. Ships so frequently disguised themselves by sailing under false colours that it was rare to find anyone under his own flag. Indeed, it might have been an effective double bluff for a British ship regularly to fly British colours. She would then have been taken almost automatically for a Frenchman or a Spaniard. Cochrane, like all other captains of his day, had his locker stuffed with the flags of all the nations; but he also had ideas of his own which were new and which were to prove startlingly successful.

But he knew that guile alone would not be enough. His men must be highly trained and always alert. Since inactivity was the worst thing that could possibly befall a ship's company, his own men must be kept constantly at work, if possible in real action; if not, in practice. With his crew well trained and the *Speedy* spreading enough canvas to satisfy even him, and with his own guile, skill and daring, he felt certain that he could make his ship the terror of the coast.

In the end he overreached himself, but for a year and a half the exploits of Cochrane and his men earned them a remarkable reputation.

In their first operations, between 1800 and 1801, they captured fifty enemy ships, took five hundred prisoners and lost only one man themselves. In a very few months the enemy became so alarmed and angry that ships were specially detached from the French and Spanish navies to search out the *Speedy* and destroy or capture her. Early one morning one of these ships had the chance for which she was looking.

A passing ship had tipped off Cochrane that a large merchantman was close by. He moved steadily forward through the darkness, but when dawn was beginning to streak the eastern sky he had still found nothing. He pressed on, and then suddenly, against the still-dark outline of the coast, he saw his quarry. In the half light he could not identify her, but she certainly looked like a merchantman. He came to within hailing distance. The decks were deserted, the ship looked harmless. But just as he was preparing to send a boat across to seize her, armed men poured up from below on to the main decks and gun ports were raised, revealing row after row of gleaming barrels. The *Speedy*, it seemed, was well and truly caught by a Spanish man-of-war many times her size.

But this was something which Cochrane had foreseen. As soon as he had heard that enemy warships had been specially detailed to search for him, he decided that he would need a better disguise than the usual foreign flag. So he had looked for some neutral ship which was roughly the same size as the *Speedy* and which was well known on the coast. The ship he finally picked on was a Danish brig, the *Clomer*. He had the *Speedy* painted in her colours. He shipped on board a Danish quartermaster complete with Danish uniform. This type of camouflage was fully developed more than a hundred years later, when, in 1916, the Royal Navy produced her Q-ships—warships disguised as merchantmen—but it was little known in the early days of the nineteenth century.

As soon as Cochrane realized that he was in fact facing a greatly superior enemy ship, he at once ran up the Danish flag; but this by now was routine—it no longer impressed the Spaniards. They fired a warning shot and put off a boat to investigate.

Cochrane now played his second trick—the Danish quartermaster with his Danish uniform. The quartermaster hailed the oncoming boat in hesitant Danish-Spanish. Still the Spaniards came on, and Cochrane had to produce a third trick.

He ran up the quarantine flag and instructed the quarter-master to shout across the narrowing gap that the *Speedy* was only two days out of Tangier, and that the plague was raging there. This stopped the Spaniards dead. They easied their oars, stared at the quarantine flag and gesticulated to each other. Then, swinging round, they pulled back to their ship as though plague germs were leaping at them across the water.

As soon as the Spanish captain heard the report from his boat's crew, he told Cochrane to sail away, wished him a good voyage, and spurred his men aloft to get under sail himself.

As, with his grinning men, Cochrane watched the Spaniards preparing to get under way, one of his officers came to him.

'They've put their arms away and lowered their ports,' he said. 'The men in the rigging are an easy target. Let's have at them, sir.'

Cochrane was prepared to use any trick to outwit an enemy, but he was not prepared to kill human beings when they were sitting targets. To the exasperation of his officers and men he ordered the *Speedy* to get under way without firing a shot.

'Never mind,' he said to them. 'You'll get your chance soon enough.'

The chance was to come in a very few days, and sent the officers and men of the *Speedy* into what was probably the most remarkable fight between two ships in naval history.

It happened like this. In the late afternoon of May 4th, 1802, the *Speedy* was off Barcelona with two prizes which she had just captured. She had put some of her own men aboard as prize crews and was escorting her captures towards Port Mahon, when seven gunboats came out of Barcelona and gave chase. Cochrane did not want to risk losing his prizes, so he crowded on sail. The gunboats fired at him until he was out of range, and then returned to Barcelona, leaving Cochrane to proceed unmolested towards Port Mahon.

Cochrane was puzzled. Whenever previously he had met

Spanish gunboats, these had kept clear of him, because, small though the *Speedy* was, she was larger and more powerful than they were. Yet here were these gunboats from Barcelona actually seeking a fight. There was something odd going on. He saw his prizes well on their way to safety and turned back towards Barcelona to investigate.

He arrived there about midnight on the 5th. The gunboats were still on the watch. As he approached they fired several rounds at him, and then retreated towards the port. Cochrane got near enough to one of them to launch a broadside at her, but at that two others who were sailing inshore swung round and came into the attack. One of them got in a shot which severely damaged the famous foretopgallant yard. Although the *Speedy* was now badly handicapped, the gunboats did not try to press their advantage, but instead swung round again and made for the safety of the port. This was very odd indeed.

The *Speedy* put out to sea, and spent the whole of the next day in repairing the damaged yard and rigging. But while the repairs were being made, Cochrane thought over the behaviour of the Spanish gunboats. What could it mean? The gunboats had not been willing to risk a full engagement, but on the other hand they had not immediately run away. They had only retreated towards the port after they had fired at the *Speedy*. Were they trying to entice her into a trap? Was something lying concealed just inside the harbour which would put an end to the *Speedy*'s depredations if only she came within range?

Cochrane had already decided to find out for himself, and spent the day guessing what sort of trap was prepared for him, and making plans to deal with whatever he should find.

Then, after he and his men had had some hours of sleep, they came slowly towards the harbour just before daylight on May 7th. The gunboats were waiting for him. He passed one, then another. They did not fire. Two more were at the entrance. When they saw him coming they turned round and moved slowly inshore. Cochrane followed.

And thus, just as dawn was breaking, he came round a headland and saw what it was all about.

In the far distance, scarcely visible in the dawn, small ships lay at anchor; but in the foreground, clearly visible and under sail, was something which the headland had prevented him from seeing. This was *El Gamo*, a large Spanish frigate. Cochrane found himself broadside on to her guns.

He saw at once how serious his position was. *El Gamo* was 600 tons against the *Speedy*'s 158 tons. Besides two twenty-four-pound carronades which fired grape-shot, she had thirty twelve-pounder and eight-pounder guns, firing a broadside of 190 pounds, against the *Speedy*'s twenty-eight. The range of her guns was a thousand yards, against the *Speedy*'s one hundred. She was manned by a crew of 319, whereas the *Speedy*, because so many of her men had been put aboard her prizes, was down to fifty-four. It was as though the smallest of corvettes with only half her complement were suddenly to be faced by a fully manned enemy cruiser.

Although Cochrane had prepared plans down to the minutest detail for dealing with just such a situation, the fight might conceivably have been over within sixty seconds. The Spanish guns could pound him without risk of reply. But for some reason the Spanish captain hesitated to fire. Because of her disguises, the *Speedy* was not easy to identify with absolute certainty. She might possibly be another

Spanish ship; she might be a French ally; she might be a neutral. Cochrane, of course, added to the uncertainty by at once running up American colours. And while the Spaniard still hesitated, he sailed fast across the harbour. When at last the Spaniard came to a decision and let loose his first broadside, Cochrane for the moment was out of range and safe. He was now ready to fight the battle according to his own plans.

Obviously it was useless for the *Speedy* to fire at any range above a hundred yards. Equally obviously, so long as the range was more than a hundred and less than a thousand, she could be hit repeatedly without any chance of replying. Cochrane knew that he must swing round and get to within a hundred yards before the Spaniards had time to re-shot their guns or themselves to swing round and bring their other broadside to bear. He did his best to keep clear of either broadside by coming at *El Gamo* as nearly as possible head on.

For several tense minutes he bore down on the enemy. His men stood to their guns under orders not to fire until their captain gave the word. They peered through the growing light towards the enemy guns, which they felt might at any moment come to bear with devastating effect on them. By his skill at the helm, countering every move the Spaniard made, Cochrane kept the *Speedy* head on as the gap narrowed between them.

At last, without giving *El Gamo* a chance for another broadside, he had come within range, and his men looked up expectantly for the order to fire. It did not come. Cochrane sped on. He was down to eighty yards, to sixty yards, to forty yards. Now he was right under *El Gamo*'s lee, and with a sudden twist of the helm managed to lock the *Speedy*'s

26

yards in the Spanish rigging. Then, and only then, at a distance of a few feet, he gave the order to fire.

The effect surprised him. He had given orders that his guns should be double-shotted, but in their eagerness the *Speedy*'s officers had treble-shotted them, and the first discharge at almost point-blank range tore into the enemy's main deck and killed several men. Cochrane could well have foreseen some casualties, but he could never have foreseen that his very first broadside would kill, among others, both the enemy captain and the enemy bo'sun.

The shock of this first broadside was considerable. But *El Gamo* quickly recovered, and as her guns were now re-shotted she was able to fire her second broadside. But her deck was a good ten feet higher than the *Speedy*'s, so the shots passed through the rigging killing no one and doing little damage. On the other hand, the *Speedy*, elevating her guns, was able to cause havoc on the enemy main deck. She launched a second broadside.

The Spaniards realized that if this went on, though they might be able to damage the *Speedy*'s rigging and even dismast her, their own ship would quickly become untenable. There was only one thing for them to do. They must leap down on to the *Speedy*'s decks and take her by hand-to-hand fighting.

'Prepare to board!'

Despite the noise of the firing, this order was clearly heard on the *Speedy* and Cochrane reacted at once. A party of his men were standing ready with spars in their hands.

'Bear off!' shouted Cochrane, and at the order spars from the *Speedy* were forced against *El Gamo*'s sides, and the narrow gap of water between the two ships suddenly widened. Boarding for the moment was impossible.

27

Worse, the Spanish seamen ready to board had come pouring up from below on to the main deck. They were easy targets for the *Speedy*'s elevated guns. A broadside at once crashed into them. Seeing some of their comrades killed, and seeing that the gap between the two ships was now too wide for a jump, the Spaniards dashed down again to their guns, which, when depressed, could now hit the *Speedy*.

At once Cochrane brought his ship again alongside, and the Spaniards' broadside could do no more than cut his rigging. Again the Spaniards tumbled breathlessly up the companionways to the main deck ready to board. Again Cochrane gave the order 'Bear off!' and again his broadside crashed into the assembled boarders.

Their casualties were now mounting. The idea of boarding was abandoned. They went back to their guns and fired round after round into the *Speedy*'s rigging.

Cochrane looked at the damage. It was not yet severe, but another hour of this and the *Speedy* might be unsailable. So he prepared for his major assault.

'Lads,' he shouted, 'we must either take this frigate or be taken ourselves, and you know the Spaniard gives no quarter. Put your backs into it for a few minutes and we will win.'

The crew knew already what they had to do.

Cochrane and his first lieutenant, Parker, with the bulk of the crew, were to leap aboard *El Gamo* in the middle of the ship, or waist. A smaller number, blackening their already dirty faces with soot, were to climb up by the chains to the forecastle and attack from there. Only one man, the ship's doctor, Guthrie, was to remain on board, in charge of the helm. As Cochrane gave the order, Guthrie closed the gap between the two ships and brought the *Speedy* alongside.

Cochrane and Parker leapt up the waist and on to the main deck, followed by the main party of boarders. Simultaneously the smaller party clambered to the forecastle and suddenly appeared through the smoke, their black faces looking particularly horrible. Seeing these, the superstitious Spaniards for a moment stood transfixed, believing that they were beset by devils, and during these moments of indecision Cochrane and his men laid about them for all they were worth.

This trick of Cochrane's gave his men a momentary advantage, but the Spaniards recovered and fought with great gallantry for several minutes. Cochrane then played yet another trick. Seeing the Spanish flag still flying from the masthead, he ordered one of his men to haul it down, whereat some of the Spanish crew, believing that their colours had been struck by order of their own officers, laid down their arms and surrendered. Others, however, continued fighting, so Cochrane ran to the side and shouted to the *Speedy* to send at once another fifty men as reinforcements. As the doctor was the only man aboard and he was in charge of the wheel, this was a particularly outrageous piece of bluff, but it was effective. Those who had continued fighting now gave in, and Cochrane at once ordered the 263 Spaniards who were still unhurt to go down into the hold, pointed the Spanish guns down the hatchway with his own men standing over them with lighted matches, put another thirty of his men on board as a prize crew, and took his prize safely into Port Mahon. In the action *El Gamo*'s losses were her captain and fourteen others killed and forty-one wounded. This was more than the total ship's company of the *Speedy*. The *Speedy* herself lost three killed besides seventeen wounded, among whom was the first lieutenant, Parker.

Such was Cochrane's first great sea fight. It was hailed at the time by fellow officers as the greatest achievement ever accomplished by a single ship. Naval historians today agree with that judgment, but immediately it brought Cochrane little credit with Admiralty. Indeed, it helped to land him in trouble which threatened to end his naval career.

3. Sea Harvest

FOR SUCH AN EXPLOIT as the capture of *El Gamo*, Cochrane would normally have been promoted post-captain at once. Unfortunately, news of it was delayed on its way to London, and in the meantime Admiralty received some details of a later, and seemingly less creditable, event.

At about four o'clock one July morning two months after *El Gamo*'s capture, Cochrane was convoying a small packet. Suddenly there was a shout from the look-out:

'Three ships astern, sir.'

Cochrane went at once to the masthead.

'H'm,' he said. 'I'd like to think those were galleons from South America. But I doubt it. Damn this light. We'll have to close to get a better look.'

The *Speedy* swung round to keep herself between the newcomers and the packet in her charge. She began cautiously to narrow the gap between herself and the oncoming ships.

Cochrane kept his telescope almost continuously to his eye, trying to pierce the half-light.

'I believe those three are Frenchmen,' he said suddenly. 'Look at their rigging.'

It was still too dark to be sure. But it was disturbing that the French ships kept on course. If they were only merchantmen, surely they would tack away from possible danger?

At last Cochrane lowered his telescope. 'Those are line-of-battle ships,' he said quietly, 'not merchantmen at all. Go about!'

The *Speedy* had beaten a ship four times her size, but she could not hope to beat three ships, each of them ten times her size. Her crew sprang to the rigging, and as she went about again they crowded on all sail and beat to windward.

Then the wind dropped.

The *Speedy*, with her comparatively small spread of canvas, could make little headway in the now light air. The Frenchmen too were slowed, but their greater spread of sail helped them to keep way on. They narrowed the gap at what seemed an alarming rate. Cochrane, despairing of sail, tried to 'sweep' with cumbersome oars thrust over the side. But the Frenchmen still gained.

'Throw the guns overboard!'

To the sound of heavy splashes the *Speedy* was turned to sail before such wind as there was, but even though she was now lightened she could not get away. The Frenchmen parted on different tacks, so as to keep her constantly in reach of one or the other. Whichever was nearest now began to fire broadsides as she passed in tacking, and cut the *Speedy*'s rigging severely, still further reducing her speed.

None the less, for three hours, tacking now this way and now that, Cochrane managed to keep the *Speedy* clear of the murderous broadsides which threatened her while his charge, the packet, slowly disappeared in the distance. But he himself could not escape. Although the Frenchmen still could not get close enough to him for the kill, it seemed only a matter of time.

'Throw all stores overboard!'

With the burden of his ship now reduced to a minimum, Cochrane prepared for a last desperate throw. He would try to cut between the three Frenchmen. There was just a hope that because she was smaller and easier to manage than the heavy line-of-battle ships, the *Speedy* might widen the distance and perhaps escape while they were swinging round.

Watching intently until the nearest enemy was before his beam, he bore up and began his run. For a time, a very short time, it looked as though he might succeed, but one of the French ships, the *Dessaix*, immediately tacked in pursuit, and within an hour was so close that musket fire could carry the distance between the two ships. At that almost point-blank range, she let fly a complete broadside of round and grape. It was obvious that she intended to sink the *Speedy* with a single blow.

Luckily, in turning to bring her broadside to bear, the *Dessaix* answered her helm too rapidly, and the shot, instead of striking amidships, plunged into the water immediately ahead of the *Speedy*'s bows. But for this, the *Speedy* must inevitably have been sunk. As it was, scattered grape-shot so riddled her sails and rigging that she was left virtually helpless.

The *Dessaix* now backed again for the kill. One more broadside at the sitting target would do it. Rather than wait for his ship, his men and himself to be sent to the bottom, Cochrane at last hauled down his colours.

He was taken aboard the *Dessaix*, and offered his sword to

33

the captain. But the captain bowed to him with great politeness and said: 'I will not accept the sword of an officer who has struggled for so many hours against impossibility. Though you are my prisoner, will you please continue to wear your sword?'

Cochrane stayed aboard the *Dessaix* for some days and was still aboard when she and other French ships had a sharp brush with a British squadron. Soon he was exchanged for a captured French officer and was shipped back to England, grieving for the wonderful crew which he was now powerless to help.

*   *   *

Meanwhile, some of Cochrane's relatives had heard of *El Gamo*'s capture and began to urge his promotion on the First Sea Lord. They chose the wrong man.

John Jervis, Earl St. Vincent, was by nature cold and stern. He had had long experience at sea. After the mutinies at Spithead and the Nore, he had set himself to restore naval discipline, and now that he was at Admiralty, he was determined to break the corruption which surrounded the Navy. He was the last man to listen to the representations of interested relatives. In any event, although by now he had received full details of the *El Gamo* capture, he would not agree to the promotion of her captain until the loss of the *Speedy* was satisfactorily explained. Only when St. Vincent was satisfied about this did Cochrane receive the promotion he had earned.

Cochrane knew nothing of the reasons why, quite rightly, St. Vincent had delayed. He only saw that the promotion came three months later than he could reasonably have expected, and the loss of three months' seniority was then, as

34

now, a serious matter for an ambitious young naval officer. He was furious, and instinctively leapt into action. In so doing he showed, not for the last time, that there was a strong contrast between his behaviour at sea, when the welfare of his men was at risk, and his behaviour ashore, when nothing was at risk except his own interests.

At sea he was remarkably cool. A contemporary naval historian said of him: 'Before he fired a shot he reconnoitred in person, took soundings and bearings, passed whole nights in the boats, his leadline and spy-glass incessantly at work.' Whenever he could he planned his attacks for days ahead, reconnoitring coasts or harbours, finding out all there was to be known about his prospective enemy. At sea he did nothing without careful thought.

Even ashore he was usually mild-mannered and kindly. Miss Mitford, the novelist, once saw him at Cobbett's house; ' . . . in the very height of his warlike fame, and as unlike the common notion of a warrior as could be. As gentlemanly, quiet, mild young man was this burner of French fleets as one should see in a summer day. He lay about under the trees, reading Seldon on the Dominion of the Seas, and letting the children (and children always know with whom they may take liberties) play all sorts of tricks with him at their pleasure.'

But behind this mild manner, there was a temper which went with his red hair; and with the temper an obstinate recklessness which, ashore, blinded him to discretion.

The temper was roused now. His own promotion was late. At least as bad, so he thought, Lieutenant Parker, his first lieutenant, who had been seriously wounded in the capture of *El Gamo*, was not promoted at all. Cochrane wrote tersely to St. Vincent on Lieutenant Parker's behalf, and, getting no reply, he wrote a second time.

This time St. Vincent did reply. He said: 'It was unusual to promote two officers for such a service—besides which, the small number of men killed on board the *Speedy* does not warrant the application.'

This maddened Cochrane, and with some cause. One of his greatest virtues as a ship's captain was to see that his men were never exposed to avoidable dangers. Captain Marryat, who sailed with him as a midshipman, wrote: 'I never knew anyone so careful of the lives of his ship's company as Lord Cochrane, or anyone who calculated so closely the risks attending any expedition. Many of the brilliant achievements were performed without the loss of a single life, so well did he calculate the chances.'

Cochrane felt it his pride and duty to look after his men in every possible way, and St. Vincent's slighting reference to the *Speedy*'s small losses was stupid. But the reply which Cochrane then sent was inexcusable—unless, of course, he was prepared to sacrifice his career then and there. For this young man of twenty-six, who had only just been promoted captain, wrote to the First Sea Lord: 'His Lordship's reasons for not promoting Lieutenant Parker are in opposition to His Lordship's own promotion to an earldom as well as that of his flag captain to a knighthood: for in that battle from which His Lordship derived his title there was only one man killed on board his own flagship, so that there were more casualties in my sloop than in His Lordship's line-of-battle ship.'

A letter like that today would mean immediate court martial. For Cochrane it meant unemployment on half-pay for a time, and when, unabashed by his own effrontery, he continued to bombard St. Vincent with requests for a ship, he was at last handed the command of an old hulk, a converted collier called the *Arab*, and was sent in her to the

Orkneys with instructions to guard the fishing fleet. There was no fishing fleet in the Orkneys. Cochrane was left to cool off in useless idleness.

If St. Vincent had remained First Sea Lord, Cochrane would have remained in the Orkneys; but in December 1804, when St. Vincent had been replaced by Lord Melville, Cochrane was at last given command of a ship after his own heart. This was a brand-new frigate, the *Pallas*, a name which was soon to be circled in laurels of gold.

*   *   *

The *Pallas* was 667 tons, compared with the *Speedy*'s 158 tons, and carried twenty-six twelve-pounder guns on her main deck and twelve twenty-four carronades elsewhere, compared with the *Speedy*'s miserable armament of fourteen four-pounders.

Unlike the *Speedy*, however, the *Pallas* had no crew, and Cochrane could not attract one by a recent record of high prize money, for of course in the Orkneys the *Arab* had captured no prizes at all. So, for the first and only time in his life, he used the press gang. In his own *Autobiography of a Seaman* he writes: 'Having however succeeded in impressing some good men to whom the matter was explained'—he presumably told them how much the *Speedy* had won in prizes and why the *Arab* had won nothing—'they turned to with great alacrity to impress others, so that in a short time we had an excellent crew.' In fact he only managed to get some of his crew after a sharp clash with the constables of Plymouth, an exploit which cost him £380 18s. 10d. in fines. However, by one means or another he did manage to get his men, and sailed away for the Azores, with instructions to intercept and take ships making the run between Spain and

South America. The cruise was to last only a month, but during that time he operated so skilfully that he caused a sensation of an altogether pleasanter kind in Plymouth.

His first capture was the *Carolina* from Havana, carrying sugar and logwood. He sent her in to Plymouth with a message that in due course he would fulfil the promise made publicly to any men who joined his ship that he would fill their pockets with Spanish 'pewter' (ingots) and 'cobs' (dollars).

He did keep his promise. Prisoners from the *Carolina* told him that their ship was part of a large convoy. He began to search for this convoy, caught another of its members, this time carrying jewels, gold and silver, as well as a valuable cargo, and sent that too into Plymouth.

Two days later he came on a large ship scurrying before the wind for all she was worth. She was a Spaniard, and Cochrane stopped her with a shot across the bows. When his boat's crew boarded her, she was found to be carrying 450,000 dollars' worth of gold, the equivalent of £132,000. The boat's crew came back to the *Pallas* with this wonderful news and also with the captain of the captured ship, *La Fortuna*, and his only passenger.

Cochrane greeted the two prisoners as they came over the side, but to his astonishment they both burst into tears.

'These golden dollars,' said the captain, wringing his hands and rolling his eyes, 'among them are the whole of my life's savings.'

At that, the passenger broke in:

'And my life's savings are in them too. I've worked for seven years in the heat of South America, and was going home to Spain to spend the rest of my days in peace, and now it's gone, all gone.'

'That's not all,' said the captain. 'This isn't the first time

I have lost my fortune. Six years ago I was coming home with enough to last me for the rest of my life, and one of your British ships took me and all my fortune.'

Cochrane looked at the unhappy faces of the two men before him. Was their story true? Or was it just a line shot at an officer who looked inexperienced and soft? True or not, the story touched him. He wanted to give the men back at least some of their money. But his crew were partners in the enterprise. They shared in all prizes the *Pallas* took. Cochrane turned to the hard-boiled men who served with him and told the sad story of the two Spaniards.

'How say you?' he asked. 'Shall we return five thousand dollars each to these two men?'

Almost unbelievably, the crew shouted back: 'Aye, aye, my Lord, with all our hearts!'

At the end of the month, Cochrane returned to Plymouth with £75,000 as his own personal share in prize money, and with three five-foot golden candlesticks lashed to his masts to show the people of Plymouth what the *Pallas* could do.

But he was not allowed to keep either the candlesticks or the whole of his prize money. Customs officials told the infuriated captain that he must pay full duty on the candlesticks. He refused, and although they were of exquisite workmanship he broke them into small pieces and passed them in as old gold, which was duty free.

As for the prize money, half of it was taken from him by the Port Admiral, Sir William Young, on the technical grounds that Cochrane was working under his orders. However, he was lucky to get anything at all, for on his way home he nearly lost the whole of his newly acquired wealth and his ship. He managed to save both only by supremely skilful seamanship.

He had left the Azores behind, and was cruising through a haze which covered the surface of a sea but left the masthead of the ship in clear air. Suddenly the look-out at the masthead shouted: 'Sail on the horizon astern of us, sir!'

Cochrane, as usual, at once climbed to the masthead himself, telescope in hand. He peered towards the horizon. There certainly was sail. Three ships by the look of it, and large ones at that, he wouldn't be surprised.

He thought back to that early morning when, from the masthead of the *Speedy*, he had seen three ships astern and had hoped they were merchantmen. He was not going to take that risk again, and perhaps lose the golden treasure in his holds.

He kept on his course with all sails set. The strange ships astern also kept on their course, and grew larger.

Cochrane climbed again to the masthead. The strangers were flying no colours, but as he looked he could make out their rigging. They were clearly French.

'My God!' said Cochrane. 'They're line-of-battle ships. Have we to go through all that again?'

He altered course to get full advantage of the wind. It was now blowing hard, and a heavy sea was running. The *Pallas* heeled over until the guns of the lee main deck were continuously under water. But the three line-of-battle ships still gained.

The *Pallas* just had to put on more sail. But if she put on more sail in that high wind, her mainmast might snap.

'Get every hawser in the ship up to the mainmast,' he shouted. 'Rig them up as stays and then heave taut.'

These makeshift stays would give the mast added strength. Cochrane then set every stitch of sail, and the *Pallas* drove so deep into the waves that not a gun could be fired.

But still the line-of-battle ships came up. Soon one was on either side, less than half a mile away, and one slightly astern. The only comfort was that the Frenchmen too were heeled over so that their guns could not be fired either.

But it was clear that the *Pallas* could not outsail them, and sooner or later, when the wind abated, and the ships returned to an even keel, she would be at the mercy of their broadsides.

Since he could not outsail them, he decided to try and out-general them. In landsmen's terms, he would stop suddenly, turn round in the heavy sea, and set off again in the opposite direction. Because the Frenchmen were large and unwieldy, and because they would certainly be taken by surprise, the *Pallas* might possibly put miles of ocean between her and them before they could tack in pursuit.

This was, in fact, the trick with which, unsuccessfully, he had tried to save the *Speedy*. Would it succeed with the *Pallas*? Could that mast stand the strain?

There was nothing for it but to take the risk, unless he was prepared to lose both his ship and his treasure.

'Lads,' he said above the noise of the wind, 'I'm going about. When I say the word, take in all sails and do it on the instant. Get ready!'

His men stood to. Then, at a word, as though the crew were performing at a regatta in some calm harbour, the sails shrivelled on the yards. At once the *Pallas*, which a moment before had been heeled over at an angle of forty-five degrees, swung on to an even keel. Her speed dropped, and Cochrane put her helm hard over. Shaking from stem to stern when thus suddenly brought up and forced to cross the trough of the sea, the *Pallas* turned about. Then, literally for all they were worth, her crew once more set all sail and away she went on the opposite course.

Her enemies were caught completely by surprise. They shot past at full speed, and ran on for several miles before they could shorten sail, so that the *Pallas* went away from them at a rate of knots. By the time they had managed to get themselves on the opposite tack and renew the chase, night was falling.

In the dusk Cochrane tried yet another trick. He lowered a lantern fastened to a ballasted cask and set it adrift.

'Let's see if the Frenchies will follow that red herring,' he said.

That night no one aboard the *Pallas* slept. There were continual changes of course. The ship heaved and shuddered. The wind roared into the sails. The slightest creak of the rigging seemed like a mainmast snapping. Exhausted as they were, every man was held awake with thoughts of the morning and what it might bring. At last touches of light began to spread across the sea, and the whole ship's company peered and strained. The dawn broke and soon it was day. There was nothing but spray, green water and sunlight. They had escaped.

*　　　*　　　*

After this cruise, Cochrane and the *Pallas* were sent on convoy duties. This turned out to be peaceful work; but even when there was no enemy in sight and little likelihood of an enemy even beyond the horizon, Cochrane kept himself continually alert.

One thing about the work had particularly exasperated him. He found it almost impossible to keep his convoys together during the night. Indeed, after one crossing of the Atlantic, he arrived in port with only one ship of the convoy he was supposed to be protecting actually in sight—and that ship was attached to the *Pallas* by a tow-rope.

'It's these damned lights of ours that are the trouble,' he said. And, indeed, the lights then carried by British men-of-war were so dim that no one could see them at more than a few yards' distance.

Cochrane set himself to design a more effective lamp, which would give the merchantmen in convoy a chance to mark, follow and keep up with the man-of-war which was leading them.

When he had perfected his lamp, he sent it up to Admiralty; but after his rudeness with St. Vincent, and his even greater rudeness about Admiralty incompetence, he had few friends there. His lamp was rejected.

However, the reports which not only Cochrane but other convoy captains besides had sent to Admiralty about the difficulty of keeping their ships together probably decided Admiralty officials that, although they would not admit it publicly, Cochrane was right about the lamps. Admiralty therefore decided to offer a prize of £50 for the best-designed lamp which might be submitted to them.

Cochrane soon heard of this competition, but he suspected that it would not be worth while to send in an entry himself. So he arranged for his own lamp to be submitted in the name of his agent. Although it had previously been rejected, it now received the prize. When, however, Admiralty discovered that the designer, in fact, was Cochrane, the lamp was never used, and convoyed ships continued to lose themselves for another ten years or so, until Sir Humphry Davy, making only slight adjustments to Cochrane's design, at last persuaded Admiralty to catch up with the needs of the time.

During the long days at sea, Cochrane also experimented

43

with kites, to see if they would increase the sailing speed of his ship. Unfortunately, at the time, he had only one type of kite aboard, and though he did increase his speed with it he found that he lost much of his control over the ship. He did, however, manage to use kites in actual warfare, though in a different way from the one he originally intended.

The British Government was experimenting with an elementary form of propaganda warfare, and to their intense annoyance ships' captains were instructed from time to time to take on board large quantities of leaflets, which they were supposed to distribute in enemy countries. Generally, such leaflets remained to rot in the ship, because the only way of distributing them was to row ashore and deliver them by hand. And as the people for whom the leaflets were intended were usually hostile, the leaflet-bearers were likely to be shot.

Cochrane received his share of these leaflets when he was setting off to patrol the French coast. Like his colleagues he had no intention of letting his men risk their lives by acting as postmen. But, unlike them, he did not see why the leaflets should be entirely wasted.

'Kites! That's the answer. They'll deliver the leaflets all right, and it doesn't matter if they *are* shot,' he said.

The leaflets were brought on deck, split up into small bundles, and tied with string. The string was then attached to small kites. Then, when all was ready, and the wind was in the right direction, slow matches were attached to the retaining string and set alight.

'Let go kites!' shouted Cochrane.

At once what looked like a flock of long-legged birds rose majestically from the decks of the *Pallas*, and began to drift steadily inshore, leaving small vapour trails behind them.

They drifted across the coast and far inland, while the slow matches burned away. At last the fire reached the string, burned through it and then a cloud of leaflets descended on the countryside, to the intense irritation of the French Government.

Precisely the same trick was used by Lord Northcliffe in the first world war over a hundred years later to distribute leaflets over Germany.

*   *   *

Cochrane was now to be involved in two fights, each widely different from the other in nature, but both extraordinary, even for him.

One was the attack he made on the French frigate *La Minerve* in the Aix Roads. These roads, leading into the River Charente, were one of the best naturally protected anchorages on the French coast. They were studded with islands and shoals which made navigation dangerous for a stranger, though there were good deep-water anchorages for those who knew how to find them.

In addition to the natural advantages, the French had built forts on the outlying islands and elsewhere to cover the entrance and the deep-water anchorages, and in this safe harbour lay a French squadron, which from time to time dispatched fast and powerful ships to harry anything British which might come near.

Cochrane was instructed to take the *Pallas* into Aix Roads to reconnoitre, and coming into the entrance he at once sighted a large frigate which had been an especial nuisance to the British admiral in the area, and which later turned out to be the forty-gun *La Minerve*.

This ship on her own was considerably larger and carried

more guns than the *Pallas*; and she was immediately supported by two sixteen-gun brigs, while a mile or two away lay the full French squadron under Admiral Allemand. Beside all this, *La Minerve* was under cover of powerful shore batteries.

Cochrane reported back to his admiral, and anchored well off shore for the night. Then, early next morning, on May 14th, he again stood in close and made straight for the enemy. *La Minerve*, with her two brigs, at once weighed anchor and came to meet him. Cochrane waited until he was within almost point-blank range, and then, selecting one of the brigs, he dismasted her with his first broadside. That left him with the frigate, a second brig and the batteries of the Isle of Aix.

After an hour of fighting, intermittent because the *Pallas* continually had to tack in order to avoid shoals, Cochrane could see that the frigate's after sails were shot away, and that the main topsail yard of the brig had been cut through. Getting to windward of the frigate, he now crashed three quick broadsides into her. She was terribly shaken.

'That Frenchy's going to run up-river if we're not careful,' said Cochrane. 'We must board her before she gets near the squadron.' He turned to his coxswain: 'Lay us alongside as quick as you can,' he ordered.

The coxswain turned in towards *La Minerve* at full speed, but just as he came up to her *La Minerve* struck a shoal and stopped dead. The *Pallas* crashed heavily into her sides.

The shock dismantled the spars and rigging of both ships, and there they were, locked together, stopped and virtually unsailable, within easy reach of a powerful French squadron.

'Fire, lads, fire!' yelled Cochrane.

The *Pallas*'s broadside shivered *La Minerve*, and caused

such havoc in her crew that every man except one tumbled below to escape the next assault.

The exception was the French captain. While the balls crashed around him, he stood unmoving on deck, and then, as the British seamen re-shotted their guns, he calmly drew his pistol and fired three times. That done, he took off his hat and bowed to Cochrane. Cochrane duly took off *his* hat and bowed back.

But he knew that this was no time for further courtesies, for, looking up-river, he saw that two new frigates, both larger than the *Pallas*, had now detached themselves from the squadron and were coming downstream to help *La Minerve*. In her present damaged state, these odds were too great for the *Pallas*. *La Minerve* was aground, hopelessly crippled, and virtually in his hands. But if he now boarded her, his crew and his ship would almost certainly be captured by the oncoming frigates.

'It's no use. We must bear off,' he said; and with his crew ramming whatever spars they could find against *La Minerve*'s side, he extricated the *Pallas* and limped slowly away with what sail he could raise, towards the safety of the British fleet outside the roads.

In this action he had outfought and crippled a frigate much larger than his own, which was protected by two brigs and a shore battery. He did this in the face of a complete French squadron. His total casualties were one killed and five wounded.

*   *   *

The other action was double-barrelled and even more remarkable. After the *Pallas*'s first cruise round the Azores, Cochrane at his own expense had fitted out an eighteen-oared

47

galley. He intended to use this for cutting out ships at anchor when there was not enough wind to allow the *Pallas* herself to sail close inshore.

The galley was an immediate success, and soon became terrifyingly notorious along the French coast. Cochrane used to lower her at dead of night, and she moved so silently through the darkness that she came on her victims before the look-outs heard or saw her. As her fame grew, it did not seem to matter even if she *was* seen or heard, for at the first sign of her the crews in the smaller enemy ships leapt into their own boats and pulled for the shore without putting up a struggle of any kind.

Cochrane now planned to use her in a special operation. He had recently nosed into the River Garonne, and there had seen some French corvettes lying at anchor, with one corvette apart from the rest as a guardship. He decided to steal this corvette as a fox might steal a goose.

Waiting until it was pitch dark, he brought the *Pallas* in close, until she was just short of the Cordonan lighthouse, and anchored. He then lowered the galley and his other boats, and manned them with the whole of his ship's company, apart from forty men. He himself stayed on board the *Pallas*.

The boats put off. Silently they slid into the harbour, which was now shrouded in fog. Then, at 3 a.m., there was a whisper in the leading boat.

'There she is!'

They were alongside the guardship.

Without a further word, the men boated their oars and drifted stealthily alongside. Then, as one man, they leapt aboard, and so surprised the French seamen that they had no time to man their fourteen guns. With pistol a nd cutlass the corvette was taken inside five minutes. But the noise of the short struggle had carried across the water.

Lieutenant Haswell, who was in charge of the galley, looked through a break in the drifting fog and saw that two of the other French corvettes had weighed anchor. They had heard the fighting and were swinging down to investigate, and, if necessary, to attack.

'Get to the guns, lads!' he shouted, and at the order British seamen leapt to the French guns, and fired round after round at the oncoming French corvettes. These were driven off, and when the tide turned Cochrane's men were in comparative safety, in charge of their prize.

It was now daylight, and Cochrane was waiting at single anchor for the return of his boats with their prize, when suddenly three new enemy ships came into view. They, too, were French corvettes.

Cochrane was in a difficult position. His ship, it was true, was larger than any single corvette, but it was not, at least on paper, anything like a match for three of them, even if he had had a full complement on board; and at the present moment his crew had temporarily been reduced from 215 to a mere forty. But he had to do something.

'If these corvettes get into the river, they'll have our boats in no time. And the prize as well.' Even more important, they would have the greater part of his ship's company.

Cochrane decided on a gigantic bluff. If only he could suddenly unfurl a cloud of canvas, the enemy might think that they were facing a large, fully manned ship. After all, though it was daylight, they were still at a distance. His sails, of course, were furled as he lay at anchor. It was hopeless in the ordinary way to expect his skeleton crew to unfurl more than a few of them at a time, but he hit on a brilliant idea. He sent his men aloft with balls of thin yarn.

'Tie that round the sails,' he said, 'and then let them go one by one.' When this was done the sails remained precariously held by the yarn.

'Out knives,' said Cochrane. 'And when I say cut, cut through the yarn.' Then, weighing anchor, he shouted 'Cut!'

On the instant, the sails fell into position with all the precision of a peacetime manœuvre, and at the sight the three French corvettes swung round and made off along the coast, with the *Pallas* and her forty men in pursuit.

'We'd better give them something to think about,' said Cochrane.

He did not want them to have time to inspect his ship and see how few men there were aboard, or how slowly all subsequent manœuvres would have to be carried out.

'Man the bow guns!'

In fact, there were not seamen enough to man any other guns.

'Fire!'

Cochrane peppered the nearest retreating Frenchman, and as he narrowed the range the shots began to take effect. This was too much for the French captain. He turned inshore and deliberately ran his ship aground, dismasting it in the process. He then leapt into his boats with his crew, and pulled ashore.

'By God!' said Cochrane. 'If that captain had pulled for us instead of for the shore, he'd have captured the ship.'

The *Pallas* hove to and riddled the wreck, to make sure that she would not be able to float off on the tide. But when they saw that the chase had stopped, the two remaining corvettes turned round again and headed for the river mouth.

Cochrane at once attacked the nearest with his bow guns. Once again the captain, apparently more discreet than brave, ran his ship aground and took to his boats.

Cochrane felt that it was now high time to return to the Garonne to pick up his own boats. But as he neared the river, there was the third and last corvette scudding for home.

'We must stop that little Frenchy,' he said, and turned the *Pallas*'s bows for her. But he did not have to fire a shot. Once again the captain ran his ship aground and took to his boats.

Cochrane then went leisurely into the mouth of the river, picked up his own boats and their prize, and sailed off to rejoin the squadron.

On the way he fired more shots into the beached corvettes, and silenced a battery which had been hurriedly put up to protect one of them.

The net result of this operation was the capture of a fourteen-gun corvette and the wrecking of three corvettes of twenty-four guns, twenty-two guns and eighteen guns respectively, in addition to the two brigs in the river itself. His own total losses in all these actions were nil.

Looking back from a distance, one might try to explain this extraordinary action by saying that the French were cowards. But they were not. During the long wars with France one British sailor of those days after another has declared his admiration for French sailors as fighters.

The fact that three strong, fully manned fighting ships were induced to commit suicide when faced by an enemy who, in fact, for a moment was inferior in strength to any one of them, was a tribute to the genius of Cochrane. In later years, he kept at bay a British sheriff and his armed posse for six weeks by inducing them to believe that sacks of soot placed outside his house were in fact infernal gunpowder machines which would explode at a touch. No one suggested that the sheriff and his men were cowards. It was just that they knew Cochrane and were cautious.

4. Commando

WHEN THE *Pallas* put in for a refit, Cochrane transferred to the *Impérieuse*, a thirty-eight gun frigate of 1,046 tons. She had the usual twelve- and eighteen-pounder guns, but what specially excited Cochrane were two newly designed eight-pounders, placed in the bows and stern, which had a range of more than a mile. He could have done with these in Aix Roads, when those two frigates came down to help *La Minerve*. By the way, he had an idea about Aix Roads. He must write to Admiralty about it.

Meanwhile, he must collect a crew. He needed 248 seamen and thirty-six marines. Most of the seamen had transferred in a body from the *Pallas*, and he knew how to get the rest.

'Put this notice on the dockyard wall,' he ordered.

The notice read:

Wanted

STOUT, ABLE-BODIED MEN WHO CAN
RUN A MILE WITHOUT STOPPING WITH
A SACKFUL OF SPANISH DOLLARS ON
THEIR BACKS.

With his known record of prize money he filled his complement within the day.

* * *

Cochrane had time enough for working-up exercises and for actions to bring his ship to fighting pitch. His log-book in the following months was studded with terse reports of interceptions, quick solo actions and prizes. The *Impérieuse* had just reached her peak when a sudden switch in the war gave her the chance to pioneer a type of operation for which she and her captain were ideally suited, and which was imitated, but not excelled, in the two world wars of the twentieth century.

Since Trafalgar, Britain had been supreme at sea. But on land Napoleon was everywhere successful. He was master of the Continent, and seemed likely to master even Britain, not by invasion, but by strangling her trade with European countries. Despite her mastery at sea, Britain was as much on the defensive then as she was in 1940 after Dunkirk. But just as the strain was reaching a crisis, Napoleon made a serious mistake.

Hitherto, Spain had been his ally. Though the alliance was somewhat half-hearted, it was strong enough to prevent Britain from getting a footing on the Peninsula, and hence on the Continent generally. But in 1808 Napoleon announced that the throne of Spain was to be given to his brother, Joseph. The Spaniards, already restless, were struck deep in their pride. They revolted, and Britain, seizing her chance with unusual speed, sent an expeditionary force under Sir Arthur Wellesley, later Duke of Wellington, to help the revolt.

At once the land situation was transformed. So long as the Spanish forces were on his side, Napoleon could keep the British out of Spain without tying up many French troops. But after the revolt, he had to withdraw crack troops from all over the rest of Europe, not only to block the British but also to suppress the Spaniards. He foresaw clearly enough that this would weaken him in other theatres. But he could not have foreseen that his efforts to reinforce the garrisons in Spain would be prevented for weeks and delayed for months by the operation of a single British ship, the *Impérieuse*, under Cochrane.

Cochrane arrived off the north-east coast of Spain almost at the same moment as Wellesley arrived in the south. The instructions he received from his commander-in-chief, Lord Collingwood, were to interfere with the French advance into Spain, sometimes on his own, sometimes with smaller ships attached to his command, by any means he could devise. It was a job after his own heart.

He summoned his officers. 'Well,' he said, 'for once we're on a friendly coast.'

To a ship operating on its own far from base this was, of course, an enormous advantage over anything he had previously experienced. He remembered how the *Speedy*, the *Pallas* and the *Impérieuse* herself had all at one time or another run out of water. They had had to fight pitched battles before they could refill their tanks or replenish stores in hostile country. At times Cochrane had been reduced to capturing insignificant merchantmen, removing their stocks of wine, and using that not only to quench the thirst of his crew but even for ordinary washing. Now provisioning was going to be a lot easier.

'We'll be able to get what we want ashore from now on,' he said. 'Or at worst, if we can't get water that way, we'll find a river and go upstream until it's clear of salt.'

'It'll take some time to fill our tanks with buckets,' said someone.

'I have that in mind. We'll get those spare sails on deck to

55

make a tank. We can drop that overboard and haul in all the water we need.'

There were, however, still some risks about such forays ashore. Despite the revolt, the French still held strongly to some points, and had a number of mobile columns which moved between them. When landing, one could never be quite sure whether the landing party would meet friend or enemy.

As he passed Barcelona to begin his operations he fired a twenty-one gun salute in honour of the Spanish. But the salute was returned with heavy bombardment from the shore. The French obviously were in firm possession. Indeed, when Cochrane, despite the bombardment, put in closer, he could see French soldiers strolling in the streets along the quayside, but on the tops of the houses he could also see Spanish civilians waving to him and jeering at the French.

Seeing this, Cochrane said, with a grin: 'Ah well, we'll just have to be cautious.'

Supplies of water and of food did prove much easier to obtain during the forthcoming operations; though once, when he had sighted a flock of sheep near the shore and sent a landing party to requisition some much-needed fresh meat, the party so terrified the flock that it made off at high speed, and the only capture was the herdsman. Cochrane went on shore personally to apologize, and looked for his meat elsewhere.

Satisfied that, by one means or another, he could operate on his own far from base for long periods, he now turned to strategy.

'What we must do is this. Bonaparte will try to send his troops down the road from Perpignan to Barcelona. It's the only direct route. If we could block that, he would have to go miles inland, and I hear there's nothing much except cattle tracks there.'

The officers knew that road to Barcelona. They had seen it many times. It ran for miles along the coast. In places it cut along the cliff edge, with nothing but the sea on one side and rock face towering above it on the other. Blocking would be easy. Why, they could do it from the sea with those new eight-pounders.

'But don't forget that we shall not have to do it all on our own,' said Cochrane. 'The Spaniard is now on our side. We'll make his acquaintance. With a little tuition he should be a fair hand at blocking roads.'

'Resistance movement' and 'sabotage' may be relatively modern words. Perhaps Cochrane did not use them. But they exactly describe what he was planning.

There was one other thing. The French had built a chain of semaphore-signal stations right along the coast. With these they could quickly pass, not only their own orders and requests for help, but also the news of any British ship movements. The *Impérieuse* would have to attend to these signal stations.

Cochrane made them his first objective. He did not want, at any rate for the time being, to break the chain completely. He only wanted to look as though he was trying to break it. His real aim was much more subtle. It was to leave the chain in reasonable working order, but to capture a French code-signal book, so that both he and Admiral Collingwood would be able to read the messages, and so know every enemy plan in advance.

First he picked out a number of stations right on the sea coast. Then, fixing mortars in the bows of his ship's boats, he sent the boats close inshore to bombard the stations. In this way he quickly knocked out half a dozen. But it was not enough to knock out a few stations on the coast. If he was to seem in earnest about smashing the chain, he must also deal with other stations sufficiently inland to be out of range of bombardment from the sea.

He himself went ashore with a small party and began to reconnoitre. The party sighted a station well inland, and Cochrane, after studying it carefully through his telescope, decided to attack it that night.

Landing again with a slightly larger party, he completely surprised the French soldiers in charge of the station, and either killed or captured them before they could destroy the signal books. He took these under his arm, and then instructed his party to smash everything in the station, pile what would burn in a great heap, and set fire to it. He then tore a few unimportant pages from the signal books and touched them with the flames until they were charred. He then left the charred, but still recognizable, pages where they would be found next day, and retired.

He reasoned that, when the French at length returned to the station, they would see the ashes of their belongings and also the charred pages from the signal book. 'Ah,' they would say, 'these stupid English. They are such vandals that they have destroyed everything. They haven't even had the sense to keep our signal books. Look at these few pages which have escaped the fire.'

It was a long shot, but it came off. For months, both Cochrane and Collingwood were to have immediate knowledge of every French movement.

*　　　*　　　*

Cochrane then turned to the Perpignan–Barcelona road. Turning his eight-pounders at a point where it cut into the cliff face, he sent huge rocks bowling down to the road itself.

COMMANDO

Some rocks bounced off into the sea, but still left considerable craters where they had crashed. Others, rolling down
with less violence, lodged on the road, completely blocking it
for cavalry and vehicles, and making things maddeningly
difficult even for infantry.

But of course one block would be little good. The French
could clear that in a few days by levering the boulders over
the cliff into the sea. He would have to make a series of
blocks lower down.

Moving along the coast, he saw a village in which there
appeared to be no sign of the French. He landed, and was
warmly welcomed by the Spaniards. He had the ability and
the application to pick up foreign languages quickly, and was
now fluent in Spanish. He addressed the villagers with the
grandiloquence which he knew would appeal to the Spanish
mind. He made many references to their ancestors. He
recalled Spain's great history. He spoke of the bravery of the
present-day Spaniard, which, he said, he had himself
experienced in the present war.

After some time, he judged the moment ripe to come to the
matter in hand. This was the mundane matter of blowing up
roads. The Spaniards at once came down from the heights
with an eagerness which surprised Cochrane, until he found
out that they hated the French more than they feared the
devil. As soon as the revolt had broken out, the French had
changed from allies to occupiers, and had behaved with all
the ruthlessness which occupiers invariably show. The
Spaniards were now eager to do anything Cochrane could
suggest which would help them to get their own back on the
French. They needed little tuition in the art of explosives.
Within an hour, detonations were sending up showers of

stone and rubble. And when the dust settled the road was pitted with craters and blocked with debris.

Cochrane then gave his excited hearers a quick lecture on the art of guerrilla warfare, including the making of booby traps, and sailed off to another village down the coast, where he repeated the operation.

Soon the road was blocked in a dozen places between the border and Barcelona.

'Perhaps we'd better go back to see how the Frenchy is getting on farther north,' he said.

They sailed back to the point at which they had first blocked the road, and sure enough there were the French engineers hard at work. The road at this point was almost clear. Cochrane at once turned his guns on the engineers and drove them away with heavy casualties. Then he set his eight-pounders at the rocks, and within an hour the block was complete again.

He discovered, however, that while the main body of the advancing French had been held up while their engineers cleared the first block, advance parties had got round the craters, climbed over the rocks, and proceeded along the road until they found the second block, which had been made by Cochrane's friendly villagers. The advance party decided to teach these villagers a lesson.

They forced them to bring out all the furniture from their houses and all their farm implements. These were then shovelled into the craters, and all available timber was placed on top of the jumbled mass below, so that carts and horses could cross. The advance party then tossed away any spare furniture, farm implements or timber into the sea. When they had done that they burned down all the houses in the village, and went on along the road.

Cochrane discovered this when he made a new landing. He found too that the Spanish villagers, instead of being cowed, were even more wild with anger.

'Comrades,' he said to them, 'the French have treated you monstrously. They had no right to seize your property. But, if you will, we can pay them back. Your furniture and implements are now smashed in those craters. They would be useless to you even if we pulled them out. Let us pull them out and then burn them. Then, when the French come again, they will find the craters as before, but they will find nothing with which to fill them. Further, we'll blow up some more rocks, and there will be no timber with which the French can lever them into the sea.'

Perhaps because they had nothing now to lose except their lives, and because they could take care of their lives by watching for the next French arrivals and taking to the woods, the villagers agreed wholeheartedly.

By such operations as these, Cochrane and his single ship managed to hold up the advance of a complete French army for more than a month. But this was only a part of his work.

* * *

Cochrane now saw himself not only as a guerrilla commander but as a liberator, who would free his friends the Spaniards from the French. He spent days ashore instructing peasants in the art of sabotage—if ever peasants needed instruction in this particular art—contacting local commanders and working out combined operations.

He found that at nearby Mongat, a large French garrison was holding the castle which commanded the vital road. Spanish troops, assembled there in some force, had failed to dislodge this garrison, and were now settling down to a prolonged siege.

Cochrane knew that the main French force must, sooner or later, drive its way along the road, and because it was many times more powerful than the Spanish force in the neighbourhood, it would quickly raise the siege. He therefore proposed immediate action, and when this was agreed he went back to his ship.

Bringing the *Impérieuse* close inshore, he used her as a floating battery. His broadsides crashed into the walls of the fort, smashing them piece by piece to bits, and, when enough breaches had been made, the Spanish force massed, ready for a frontal assault. Seeing this, the commander of the French garrison hung out a flag of truce. He knew what he could expect if he and his men fell into the hands of the infuriated Spaniards.

Cochrane then came hurriedly ashore with a party of marines. He found that the Spaniards were ignoring the flag of truce and were advancing on the fortress. The French in their turn were firing to keep them off. Cochrane persuaded the Spaniards to hold their fire, and himself marched into the fortress at the head of his marines. There he was greeted by the commander.

'Monsieur le Capitaine,' said the commander, 'I will surrender only to you.'

He handed his sword to Cochrane, who accepted it; and thereafter gave his prisoner a ten-minute lecture about the barbaric way in which the French were now treating the people of Spain. Cochrane, the man of action, seemed to have a strange belief in the efficacy of words. He was immediately disillusioned, for, turning back from the fort, he rejoined his Spanish colleagues, told them of the surrender, and explained that the French were now his captives and would be taken aboard the *Impérieuse*. This, he said, was in accordance with the rules of warfare. The Spaniards, however, had had their homes destroyed and some of their relatives murdered. If they had heard of the rules of war, they now seemed determined to forget whatever they had heard.

Cochrane and his marines had to escort the French prisoners through lines of shouting and gesticulating Spaniards, who swung their swords whenever a French head came within reach. The extraction of these French prisoners from his Spanish colleagues was the severest part of the whole engagement.

Over and over again in the ensuing weeks, the *Impérieuse* picked out French-held forts and strongpoints and bombarded them into submission, with or without the aid of his Spanish allies.

Early one morning, Cochrane arrived off Port Vendres, and in the growing light he could see that a nearby fishing village was alive with French troops. From the activity ashore, it looked as though the village was being prepared as a transit camp and depot for the main French force, and when he took the *Impérieuse* inshore for a closer look he was greeted with a heavy bombardment from batteries which had been established there. He drew off to survey the position and think out a plan of attack.

Standing on his deck, he peered in silence through his telescope. Then suddenly he called the officer of the watch.

'Do you see what I see?'

'French cavalry are coming over the hill.'

'Yes, and behind them there's a sizeable body of infantry.'

It was true. A considerable force was descending on the village, possibly to rest and provision before proceeding south.

Cochrane could see the dust raised by the cavalry along the road, and well behind them he could see the sun glinting on the muskets of the infantrymen.

'I know how we'll deal with those fellows,' he said. 'Order our boys on deck. We'll dress them up as marines.'

Then he sent messages to two other British men-of-war which for the moment were attached to him.

The ship's boys assembled on deck in the vivid scarlet of the marines.

'I have some men's work for you,' said Cochrane. 'I'm putting you into the ship's boats and sending you off round that headland. You are not to land. We're going to play a trick on these Frenchies.'

The boys tumbled into the ship's boats as best they could in their outsize uniforms and carrying their overweight muskets. Then, when signals from the other ships showed that they too were ready, all the boats pushed off, agleam with scarlet, and moved away to the right of the village.

The French on shore could clearly see what was happening. There were a dozen ships' boats putting off, filled with scarlet uniformed marines. Obviously Cochrane intended to make a landing, and to attack the village from the south while the French infantry were still trudging down from the north. The French commander would soon settle that. At his order, the French cavalry put their spurs into their horses, galloped down the hill, raised clouds of dust as they dashed through the village streets, and pounded away up the road over the headland, and were soon lost to sight. The British marines would get more than they bargained for the moment they set foot on shore.

Cochrane watched the French cavalry gallop away and disappear, and when the last of them had vanished and the

64

dust was beginning to settle, he brought the *Impérieuse* rapidly inshore, and then let loose his broadsides at almost point-blank range against the village. The French batteries on the hills surrounding the village replied, but if they had depressed their guns sufficiently to trouble the *Impérieuse* they would have risked hitting their own men in the village itself. Their shots therefore tended to carry over the *Impérieuse* and Cochrane and his men were virtually unscathed.

Under cover of the smoke from his own guns, however, Cochrane now landed fifty real marines to the north of the town, and these crept up on one of the most troublesome batteries and silenced it. Meanwhile he himself continued to bombard the village.

By now, the French cavalry realized that they had been tricked. The 'marines' in the ships' boats made no attempt whatever to land. Further, the roar of guns showed that, whatever these 'marines' might be doing, the village itself really was being attacked. The cavalry swung round and galloped back to help their comrades.

Cochrane was ready for them. He had noted the exact spot where the road disappeared over the headland; he had worked out the range. Some of his guns, notably the eight-pounder in the stern, were trained on this spot. When the first returning horsemen appeared, Cochrane let fly at them with every gun he could spare and killed a large number. But the remainder pressed on, so Cochrane, still keeping his ship close inshore, swung towards them, and when they came within range of that, he plied them with musket-shot. They scattered off the road and made their way to the rear of the village by any way they could find. Cochrane then calmly collected his various boats and re-embarked his real marines.

He then ordered his first lieutenant to take the *Impérieuse* offshore, out of the reach of any further bombardment, and himself stayed close in with a number of large boats in which he had mounted guns. With these guns he cleared the beaches and silenced another battery. He then decided that it was time to withdraw.

In the action he had probably killed some hundred Frenchmen, set on fire several French ships, and reduced much of the village to rubble. His total losses were half a dozen wounded and some cut rigging.

*   *   *

Besides these set attacks, Cochrane made a whole series of diversionary raids and feints, which continually drew off detachments of the French from their main force and from their main task, which was to go south to get to grips with Wellesley. The actual destruction he accomplished, and his road blocks, seriously delayed French reinforcements. But even when he neither landed nor fired a shot, the mere presence of his ship occupied whole French regiments in dashing from one point to another wherever his attacks were threatened.

No sooner had the French occupied one position and left a small force to hold it than Cochrane would appear with his devastating guns, to rout the holding force and stir the Spanish inhabitants to insurrection. Then, when French reinforcements came panting up to this place, Cochrane would slip quietly down the coast to attack the place they had just left.

For several months he and his ship's company of 284 men played more havoc with Napoleon's armies in Spain than did the whole of the British Army under Wellesley.

*   *   *

His most vivid if not the most important single operation of his whole campaign took place in November 1808, outside the town of Rosas. This town was another strongpoint on the only road to Barcelona. It was guarded by strong walls and by a citadel inside those walls. When the revolt took place, the Spanish were in possession, but obviously the French could not afford to leave them there. So long as Rosas was in hostile hands, no considerable force could hope to reach the French-held Barcelona and so proceed farther south, and at once a small French force, sent out from Barcelona, had attacked and taken it. This force in turn was pushed out by the Spaniards, but by the time Cochrane came on the scene the French were preparing to take it again. Some six thousand men had been detailed for the operation, and were already marching on the town through Cochrane's road blocks and sporadic local Spanish resistance.

The Spanish garrison had sent urgent requests to Gerona for help, but this showed no signs of coming. In these circumstances, another British officer, Captain West, who had been helping the Spaniards with a tiny force of marines, decided that he would have to pull out. Though he was the senior, he vaguely understood that Cochrane was acting under the direct orders of Lord Collingwood, and therefore issued no orders except to his own men.

Cochrane decided to see what he could do on his own. He surveyed the town and the citadel, which was still held by Spanish forces. It would not be wise to put his men into either. When the French arrived, he and his men would be surrounded, without hope of escape, except the rather faint hope that Spanish reinforcements from Gerona would eventually arrive, and, having arrived, could beat off the

French. In the meantime, the *Impérieuse*, without her captain and a large part of her crew, would be immobilized.

No, he would keep out of the town. But there was another possibility. Outside the town there was another strongly built castle, known as Fort Trinidad. Cochrane went over to inspect it. It was a curious, three-towered edifice, built on a hillside which sloped fairly steeply up from the cliff edge and the sea below. One tower was on the cliff edge itself. This was connected to a second tower built farther up the hill. Above that, and also connected, was a third tower. This third tower, farthest up the hill away from the sea, clearly could not be defended. It was commanded by an advance French battery, which had already been established on the top of the hill. This battery was now proceeding systematically to shell the tower, and had opened a considerable breach. Thereat the defenders had withdrawn to the two lower towers, which were shielded from the bombardment by the tower above them.

When Cochrane arrived, it was known that the attacking French force was almost on the town, and the remaining defenders of the fort decided that it was useless to stay longer and withdrew behind the town walls.

Cochrane, however, was not so sure. He had a good look at the building. Its walls were exceptionally thick, and though the French gunners were bombarding with brilliant accuracy they were not being particularly destructive. True, a considerable hole had been made in the top tower, but it would take many more days and many more guns before even that was destroyed. Cochrane thought that he had a reasonable chance of holding on, at least for a few days, and in that time the relieving Spanish force might arrive. If it did not, and at last he had to evacuate, he could get his men down from the bottom fort on rope ladders over the cliff side to waiting boats.

He went back to the *Impérieuse* and called for volunteers. The whole ship's company stood forward. He picked a hundred men—some seamen, some marines—and two lieutenants. Then he set the rest of the ship's company to collect a strange assortment of gear. There were, of course, all manner of arms—mortars as well as muskets. There were shells; there were packages of explosives. These were understandable. But some of the other things were odd.

'I want every top chain in the ship loaded into those boats,' said the captain, 'and get me all the large fish-hooks you can find. Oh, and tell the cook that I want every drop of sludge from his galley.'

By now his men were used to this sort of thing, but they wondered what the old man was up to.

Then, when the ship's boats were ready, he ordered the guns to provide covering fire, which they did so effectively that the French battery on top of the hill was silenced at six hundred yards. Under cover of this, the boats put ashore, and the 102 men, with Cochrane at their head, were soon safely inside the two lower towers.

Cochrane ordered them to stow their gear in the bottom tower, and went along the connecting passages up the hill until he reached the top tower, which the French were shelling. Standing at the bottom of it, he looked up and saw the breach which the French gunners had made some sixty feet above his head.

'I suppose they'll put scaling ladders up to that breach when it's wide enough, and try to storm through it. Well, I think we can manage to surprise them.'

He sent for the ship's carpenter.

'Mr. Lodowick,' he said, 'I want all that timber we brought from the ship up here. Now, you see that hole in the tower? I want you to fix the timber just below that hole in the form of a hopper, funnelling downwards. Do you see what I'm getting at?'

'That I do, sir,' said Mr. Lodowick. 'Anyone who comes through that hole and gets on to the hopper will be funnelled to the bottom, and then he'll have a drop of forty feet or more, I should reckon. He won't be much use after that. Unless, of course, he can hold to the sides, sir.'

'I've thought of that. Why otherwise should I bring all that galley sludge ashore?'

Mr. Lodowick roared with laughter, and set to work.

By and by the hopper was complete, and then willing hands brought up the sludge and smeared the smooth planks with it. Anyone who landed on the top of that hopper would inevitably slide quickly and gracefully to the bottom, and thence crash to the base of the tower. It was not likely that any Frenchman who made that drop would have much fight left in him at the end of it. But Cochrane was not content.

'Bring up the top chains, the fish-hooks and some pick-axes.'

The chains were rigged over the hopper, round the outside of the two lower towers, and along the ramparts which connected these towers. On the chains, at short intervals, the fish-hooks were rigged, so that any enemy trying to catch hold of them would pierce his hands. This was perhaps the first example of barbed wire. When all the work was completed, Cochrane blocked the passage between the top and middle towers. Then he and his men put up their mortars and made ready for a siege.

Almost at once they were joined by a number of Irish

troops, who had been in the Spanish service but had decided that it was useless to remain in Rosas itself now that the overwhelming French force had arrived. They came into Fort Trinidad and were shown round.

The hopper lined with grease and the fish-hooks fixed to the tower walls filled then with childish glee. They were almost equally delighted by the first look at their new captain's face. Both eyes were black, and the nose seemed to be seriously out of place.

'Holy cow! And what's been a-happening to His Honour's face?'

'Can't you see he's bin a-fightin'? He looks a likely lad, that one.'

'Dat hopper be a foin trick, dat be. Mother of Jesus!'

They threw themselves into the fun.

The explanation of Cochrane's face was that, with the lack of caution which was usual to him where his own safety was concerned, he had become worried by a lull in the bombardment and had stupidly climbed to the breach just before the sludge was put on the hopper and had peered over at the moment when a round-shot hit the stonework below him. A splinter had flown into his face and forced his nose back into his mouth. He was in agony, but the ship's doctor, Guthrie—the same who once had remained alone on the *Speedy* and taken the helm during the fight with *El Gamo*—quickly patched him up until he could at least breathe normally again.

The attacking French force took the main town of Rosas very quickly. Six hours later, the relieving Spanish force arrived, and, finding the French in possession, marched away again without firing a shot. This left six thousand Frenchmen virtually free to subdue Cochrane, his 102

71

seamen and marines and his twenty or so Irishmen in their tower. They set about the job methodically.

First they established four more batteries on the hill overlooking the castle, but though they widened the breach in the top tower their shot otherwise had little effect. It was clear to them that a direct assault was needed if they were not to spend weeks in subduing this nuisance.

Inside Fort Trinidad, Cochrane and his men watched, ate and, when they could, slept, while offshore the *Impérieuse* harassed the French with heavy bombardment.

Before trying the assault, which even against 130 men might well mean considerable loss, the French sent a flag of truce. They offered Cochrane honourable capitulation, which meant that, provided he would leave the fort, he and his men, with their arms, could return to their ship. Cochrane, to the relief of his wild Irish, flatly refused, and the French resumed a heavier bombardment than ever.

On the following day the French sent another party with a flag of truce, but Cochrane suspected that this time they were merely intending to have a close look at the defences before the assault.

'Lads, throw some hand-grenades. The Frenchies are only here to spy out the land.' The 'truce' party retired hurriedly, and more batteries opened up on the fort.

No one inside was hurt, because all the men by now were keeping well down, but the breach in the top tower was steadily widened.

Cochrane and his men had now been in the fort for six days. They had landed before daylight on November 24th. It was now the dawn of the 30th.

For some reason Cochrane felt vaguely uneasy. He could not sleep. He went up to the ramparts and peered into the blackness. He could see nothing. There was no sound. But the uneasiness persisted. Perhaps the strain of waiting was beginning to tell. Suddenly he felt that he could bear the silence and the darkness no longer. Beside him was a mortar. Without aim or thought he fired it. The shell soared away into the dark, and when it landed there were sudden shouts in the narrow valley which led from the town between the hillside and the cliff to the fort. The shouts were followed by a burst of musketry fire. The well-disciplined French, fully armed and carrying scaling ladders, had been climbing through the darkness, in absolute silence, to make their assault.

The noise of the mortar, and of the shouts and musketry fire which followed it, woke the whole garrison. Every man stood to, and in the first light of dawn saw more than a thousand Frenchmen massing near the fort or right under its walls, ready to place their scaling ladders against the breach.

Seeing that they were detected, the French pressed on. They fixed their ladders against the topmost tower and began to climb.... Five, six, seven ladders clanged against the wall, and up each of them Frenchmen wriggled one after another. As the first man got to the top of his ladder he hesitated. There was just light enough for him to see the chasm-like hopper waiting for him in the interior. He hesitated, but men were pressing behind him. Any moment he would be tipped over the wall into the hopper and down into the tomb below. Under the pressure, the leaders on each ladder struggled on to the open wall of the breach and clung there. At once, the men behind them climbed the last few rungs, saw the drop, in turn hesitated, and in turn were forced to climb on to the wall. There, helpless, they were at once killed by musketry fire. But still others pressed on up the ladders to be mown down again in their turn.

73

Meanwhile, an almost solid mass of men waited at the bottom of the ladders for their turn to get their feet on the first rungs. Cochrane was ready for them, too. He had brought shells from the *Impérieuse*. These were now hanging suspended by ropes. His men quickly set fire to the shells, cut the ropes, and down dropped these heavy explosive balls into the men below. The shells were followed by hand-grenades. Dead men were seen lying in heaps at the foot of the tower, and those who were still alive drew off amid loud cheers from Cochrane and his men.

Hearing the cheers, a second body of Frenchmen, who had taken up a position with the batteries on top of the hill, assumed that the castle had fallen. They at once came running down the hill, cheering as they went, and letting off their muskets. The garrison was now free to attend to them with mortar fire and muskets. The losses of this second party were almost as heavy as the first. They retired in confusion.

Only one Frenchman remained near the castle. He was an officer who had scaled one of the ladders and had remained in the opening of the breach. He would not risk the hopper; he would not retreat down the ladder until he was sure that those of his comrades who were still alive had escaped. He was just ready to descend when he found himself covered by Cochrane armed with a musket. He was caught. There could be no escape. Dragging himself fully upright, he faced Cochrane and prepared to receive his shot. Cochrane had never seen a braver or prouder man. He lowered his musket.

'A fine fellow like you was not born to be shot down like a dog,' he said. 'As far as I am concerned you are at liberty to make the best way you can down the ladder.'

At this the French officer bowed politely, as if he had been on parade, climbed sedately down the ladder and walked leisurely away up the hill.

About two thousand French soldiers had taken part in the assault. Fifty of their bodies were found heaped at the foot of the tower. Many more dead bodies were carried away by their retiring comrades. At least as many were killed on the hillside when the second assault party came running down from the batteries. Cochrane's total losses were three killed and three wounded.

Even so, he began to wonder whether even these losses were, in fact, worth while, since a large Spanish force which had been instructed to protect or relieve the town itself had left without troubling to fire a shot.

However, for the time being he decided to hang on, in the hope that, even now, a new Spanish force would come to relieve Rosas. Meanwhile the French dropped any ideas of a second assault and contented themselves with setting up more batteries and peppering the topmost tower, thereby greatly widening the breach.

But after some days Cochrane saw that the whole French force was being positioned for a grand assault from several angles. Worse, a gale had sprung up, and, looking across the water, he could see that the *Impérieuse* was dragging her anchors. Very shortly she would have to weigh and put to sea. That would mean that his only line of retreat would be cut off. It might be a week—even longer—before the *Impérieuse* could put in again. He doubted that he could hold out that long. So, with his Irishmen still protesting, Cochrane prepared to evacuate on December 5th.

The first to be sent over the cliff down the rope ladders to the waiting boats were some Spanish stragglers, who had come into the castle late in the siege. The next were Cochrane's

Irishmen. He could not trust them to withdraw if they were left to the last. They would be busy thinking up new tricks to play on the French. After them went his own marines and then the seamen, last of all except for Cochrane and two others.

While the loaded boats pulled out to sea, and the *Impérieuse* kept up a terrific bombardment of the shore for covering fire, Cochrane and his two remaining men filled the middle and bottom towers with booby traps. All the remaining explosives were stacked together, trains were laid, and at the last moment fired. Then the rearguard of three themselves climbed down the cliff and pulled back unmolested to their ship.

The booby traps were Cochrane's only failure in the operation. One of them did indeed explode soon after he had got back on board. But the Frenchmen knew the man with whom they were dealing. Instead of rushing into the fort when they saw Cochrane leave, they prudently waited to see what he had left behind him. No one was therefore hurt by the first explosion, but unfortunately the lighted trains running on to the other mines were blown out by the force of it. So, instead of being themselves destroyed or at best being able to take possession of a heap of rubble, the French eventually marched in to a still serviceable fort.

None the less, Cochrane and his small band of men had held up six thousand French soldiers badly needed for other work for eleven days. They had killed or wounded a large number of them. It was a courageous, ingenious and highly effective operation, but it was still only one incident in the campaign which Cochrane had fought almost single-handed against the might of France.

For months he and his ship's company had been on their

own, dependent on no one for orders, relying on no one for supplies. Subject only to a general instruction that he should smash lines of communication and so prevent the French from bringing reinforcements south, Cochrane had improvised, and improvised brilliantly. His direct assaults, his diversionary raids, and the insurrections which he had stirred up behind the lines, had pegged down forces a thousand times more powerful than the small force under his own command. His efforts had made it possible for Wellesley to establish himself solidly on the Peninsula; and they had, incidentally, set a practical example of guerrilla commando tactics which were to be imitated and developed by fighting men in future wars.

For all this he received no material reward whatsoever. Indeed, on the return of the *Impérieuse* to Plymouth in March 1809, he received a reprimand from Admiralty because he had used up more sails, stores, gunpowder, shot—and no doubt fish-hooks and ship's sludge—than their Lordships thought that he should have done.

But through his actions themselves, and through the accounts of them which Marryat subsequently published, he did at least have the reward of being an example which inspired British fighting men for generations afterwards.

5. Fire in the Roads

THEIR LORDSHIPS at Admiralty were worried.

Four years ago, at Trafalgar, Nelson had hit the French fleet so hard that it had splintered in all directions. Some fragments had flown to Brest, others to Lorient, still others to Aix. Cochrane had run into the squadron at Aix already when cruising with the *Pallas*.

Because the units were scattered, because there was no longer a French fleet, Britain's transatlantic trade was safe, and the rich West Indies merchants, who fed that trade, could go to sleep without fear of waking to find Villeneuve under their beds—or at least to find his squadrons in their harbour.

But now there had been a near-disaster. Lord Gambier, in charge of the fleet blockading the French in Brest, somehow had allowed his prisoners to break out; and though he had sent Admiral Duckworth to search for them all the way down to Cadiz and on to Madeira no trace at first was found.

Then, weeks later, the truth came out. The French had burst out of Brest, sailed to Lorient and released the squadron cooped up there, and thence had got clear through to Aix, where they joined the squadron under Admiral Allemand. These three units now made a formidable fleet, which at any moment might break from Aix in the same way that two of its constituents had broken from Brest and Lorient. That would mean serious trouble. The West Indies merchants shivered in their beds; and ordinary Britons, already on scanty rations because Napoleon had cut off supplies from the Continent, saw themselves going shorter still if the trans-atlantic trade were to be cut or even interrupted. The Navy, they thought, had let them down; they were angry. When their Lordships at Admiralty happened to pass a gibbet, they instinctively felt for their necks.

Something had to be done. But what? After the break-out from Brest, Lord Gambier had come home. There was no point in hanging about there after the French had flown, was there? Anyway, he wanted to look at his estate. Their Lordships sent Lord Gambier back to duty outside Aix at once.

But he had allowed one squadron to escape already. So long as French ships were afloat, he might easily let them escape again. The French would weigh anchor while he was holding a prayer meeting.

Their Lordships shook their heads. Gambier had once been a fine frigate captain, ready to fight anyone or anything. But now he seemed to have gone soft. Perhaps it was that rich wife he had married. Broad acres and soft beds! They did not make good seamen.

Look what had happened. The man had got bored with the sea. He did not know what to do with himself during these long blockades. So he got religious mania. Well, religion was all right, they supposed. But even Nelson, who did odd things in his time, never put tracts before training.

But this fellow Gambier . . . when he should have been putting his men through gunnery practice he put them through their catechism.

Well, then, why not dismiss him? Their Lordships shrugged. Dismissal was a catching disease. The old man must be kept in his job. But he needed prodding. They must put a fire-cracker under him—not the boot. He must be told to attack, and if possible destroy, the newly re-formed French fleet.

'You are,' he was told, 'to take into your consideration the possibility of making an attack upon the enemy, either conjointly with your line-of-battle ships, frigates, small craft fireships, bombs and rockets—or separately by any of the above-named means.'

Gambier replied at once. 'The operation of fireships,' he said, 'is a horrible mode of warfare, and the attempt hazardous in the extreme.'

To send in line-of-battle ships was to expose them 'to be raked by red-hot shot etcetera' by the batteries in the Island of Aix. After a long list of such protests and objections, he added that he was prepared to obey orders 'however great the risk may be of the loss of men and ships.'

One can understand some of his objections. The French fleet was protected by a large number of guard-boats, which patrolled between them and the British. If they saw fireships approaching, the crews in these guard-boats might be able to intercept them, turn them away from their own fleet, and kill the few men who manned them. On the other hand, if line-of-battle ships were used for a direct attack, these ships would have to run past the shore batteries—there was some risk in this even when they were on the move—and might run aground either in the channel or on one of the many shoals which dotted the roads. If that happened, they could well be sitting targets, both for the shore batteries and for the French fleet.

Like Jellicoe one hundred years later at Jutland, Gambier felt that by taking risks he might lose the war in one afternoon. Would it not be better to play safe and keep the French fleet cooped up, rather than to try to destroy it?

These were serious naval considerations. But maybe he took others into account as well. He probably realized by now that his religious interests were causing considerable dissension in the fleet he commanded. Those officers who thought it wise to keep on the right side of their commander-in-chief went through the religious exercises he had set for their ships' companies and themselves. Other officers, who said that they were part of a fleet, not of a prayer meeting, refused to cater to Gambier's foibles, and promptly threw over the side the tracts he sent them for distribution among their men. They then found that this independence in matters not directly connected with the service was interfering with their promotion.

With such an atmosphere abroad, the fleet which lay off Aix was in no spirit for a great and possibly dangerous enterprise. Perhaps Gambier realized this. It at least provided him with another excuse for inaction.

Their Lordships by now were thoroughly alarmed. A half-hearted commander was half-way to defeat before the fight began. Yet something must be done. Suddenly, the First Sea Lord, Mulgrave, had an idea. Some years before, that fellow Cochrane in the *Pallas* had reconnoitred Aix, and had sent a letter suggesting that the squadron then anchored there could be burned. Cochrane was on his way home in the *Impérieuse*, wasn't he? Mulgrave sent a clerk to get the letter off the file, read it to their Lordships, and then sent a signal to Cochrane requesting his immediate presence in Whitehall.

*   *   *

Lord Mulgrave looked at the young captain before him.

'You see what the position is,' he said. 'It will never do if Allemand escapes into the Atlantic. We must attack him. The Lord Gambier will not take upon himself the responsibility for attack, and I am bound to tell you that their Lordships are not prepared to bear the onus of failure.'

He then made an extraordinary proposal.

'Will you, my Lord, plan and lead the attack yourself?'

The commander-in-chief was directly opposed to the attack. The Admiralty refused to accept responsibility for it. Even with all the help he could get, the risks in it were considerable. But would a junior post-captain, over the heads of fleet officers senior to him, over the head even of his commander-in-chief, please take the job?

Cochrane stared. 'My Lord, how can I accept?' he said. 'Lord Gambier has already condemned the attack as hazardous and desperate. He will think it presumptuous of me to undertake it after that.'

'I will make you all right with Lord Gambier.'

'But what of his officers who are senior to me? This can only excite jealousy against me in the fleet.'

'This is no time for naval etiquette. They have said that the attack is impracticable. They can't blame you if after that we give the command to someone who thinks he can succeed.'

Cochrane pulled at his side-whiskers. He was sure his plans would succeed, but really the set-up was too odd for words. It was almost incredible. Was there something behind it? He began to suspect a political trick. He was not only a serving naval officer. He was also a politician, for in those days serving officers were allowed to take part in politics, and he himself had stood for the rotten borough of Honiton. In the first election there he had announced that he would pay no bribes whatever to secure votes. Consequently he was soundly beaten. But when the result came out, he let it be known that those who had voted for him could collect £10 from his agent as a reward for withstanding the £5 bribe of the other side. In consequence, when the next election came along, he was elected by a large majority, and this time refused to pay anything into the grasping hands which were held out to him. He went into the House of Commons, and there at once began to attack the naval corruption of which he had seen so much. Further, as one of the only two reformers in the House, he made a general onslaught on the Administration of Lord Liverpool.

Now, sitting in the First Sea Lord's room at Admiralty, he remembered that Lord Mulgrave was himself a member of the hated Liverpool Administration. Could it be that Lord Mulgrave had the idea in his mind that if the attack on the French succeeded the Administration would get the credit, and that if it failed a troublesome political opponent would get the blame?

Cochrane looked into what he thought was a trap, and hesitated.

At last he said: 'My Lord, if you will, I will prepare a detailed plan of attack. But I cannot lead it myself. My health is poor. Pray give the command to someone else.'

Lord Mulgrave stared gravely at the strong, healthy figure before him and the face which glowed with the sea air.

'It's no use,' he said with a smile. 'You must go. The Board cannot listen to any further refusal.'

Within ten days the *Impérieuse* had joined the fleet off Aix.

*   *   *

Gambier himself received Cochrane aboard his flagship, the *Caledonia*, with gentlemanly courtesy, and discussed plans for the fight in some detail. But other officers in the fleet were openly and violently hostile. Cochrane had only just left the commander-in-chief and gone into a neighbouring cabin when he heard a violent commotion on deck. The commotion was raised by Admiral Sir Eliab Harvey, who had fought with great bravery at Trafalgar as captain of the *Temeraire*. He had now exploded on to the flagship to protest at Cochrane's appointment.

He went straight down to Gambier in his cabin, and said between clenched teeth: 'I wish once again to volunteer to lead the attack against the French.'

Gambier looked mildly at him and said: 'I'm sorry, Sir Eliab, but the Board of Admiralty have fixed on Lord Cochrane.'

Sir Eliab could hold himself in no longer. 'I don't care,' he shouted, now purple in the face. 'If I am passed by and Lord Cochrane or any other junior officer is appointed in preference, I will immediately strike my flag and resign my commission.'

'There is really nothing that I can do about it. These are their Lordships' orders.'

'My God, I never saw a man so unfit for a command of the fleet as you are. Instead of sending boats to sound the channels you have been amusing yourself with mustering the ships' companies. If Lord Nelson had been here, he wouldn't have anchored in Basque Roads at all. He would have dashed at the enemy at once.'

While the bewildered commander-in-chief was still gasping for breath, Sir Eliab then stumped out of the door and into the next-door cabin, where Cochrane was standing. At the sight of him, Sir Eliab momentarily calmed down. He walked across and shook hands.

'I don't mean anything personal by all that,' he said, jerking a thumb towards the cabin of the commander-in-chief. 'But,' he said, raising his voice, 'this is not the first time I have been lightly treated because I am no canting Methodist, no hypocrite, no psalm-singer, and'—here he put his mouth close to the cabin wall and bellowed—'don't cheat old women out of their estates by hypocrisy and canting.' Then, lowering his voice, he said directly to Cochrane: 'I am very sorry to have a junior officer placed over my head.'

'You must not blame me for that, Sir Eliab. But permit me to remark that you are using very strong expressions about the commander-in-chief.'

'Pooh, that's nothing. I used far stronger expressions to Lord Gambier's face in there just now.'

'I can only remark, Sir Eliab, that you have a strange notion of prudence,' said Cochrane with a smile. This, coming from a man who, as a junior lieutenant, had written that abusively insulting letter to the First Sea Lord, St. Vincent, was a choice comment. Admiral Harvey brushed it off. Stamping up the companionway, he went over the side still exploding, within easy earshot of the groups of delighted officers and men who had assembled to listen to him.

He was court-martialled and dismissed the service forthwith.

Such was Cochrane's introduction to the colleagues with

whom he was supposed to carry out the most important, and probably the most dangerous, exploit in his career to date. His reception by some other, more junior, officers was hardly less hostile. He was sad about it, but not disturbed. It gave him the excuse for going ahead with his plans on his own, which was the way he always worked best.

That very night, within a few hours of his arrival, he began to reconnoitre. Putting off from the fleet, he brought the *Impérieuse* close enough inshore to get a good view of the French. There they were—eleven line-of-battle ships moored in two lines abreast across the channel, protected to seaward by frigates, by the shore batteries of Aix to the north, and by shoals and more shore batteries to the south. At first sight their position looked impregnable.

The French admiral himself, however, was not so sure about this. He had, in fact, written to Napoleon warning him that an attack might be made. But Napoleon had pooh-poohed the idea. 'You may quiet your apprehensions that the enemy would attempt something against the Isle d'Aix. Nothing could be more insane than the idea of such an attack. I am annoyed to see you with such notions.' But Napoleon did not know the sea, and had no direct experience of Cochrane. Admiral Allemand knew both.

Cochrane spent some time inspecting the French fleet through his telescope. Then, when the light had faded, he put off in his ship's boat, and began to take soundings in the channel. Lord Gambier had told Admiralty that this channel was only a mile wide, and had argued that any line-of-battle ship passing down it must be in range of the shore batteries during its passage. Cochrane, unseen in the darkness, pulled right under the batteries, and took his first soundings. Then he began to traverse the channel, taking soundings as he went. To his delight, but not altogether to his surprise, he found that Lord Gambier was wrong. Even the largest line-of-battle ship could, with care, pass down it on the far side and be out of range of the batteries.

What were these batteries anyway? He had had a good look at them while it was still daylight, and saw that they were under repair. Anyway, it looked to him as if the guns were fixed facing north, to deal with the ships lying out to sea. Only guns facing south would be any use against ships which were actually entering the roads.

'So much for Gambier's talk about our ships being raked with red-hot shot,' he said.

As it happened, Gambier did turn out to be right on one point. During the actual attack he did at last send in a number of British line-of-battle ships, and one of them, the *Caesar*, did run aground. She had gone too far over in the channel and touched the Boyart shoal. But if Gambier had been right about the shore batteries, the *Caesar* should have been an easy target while she was on the shoal. In fact she was not hit once.

Cochrane proceeded steadily in his boat across the channel until he had convinced himself of its width. Then, instead of returning to the *Impérieuse*, he told his men to pull cautiously nearer to the French. For some time, with their oars muffled, they rowed in silence.

Suddenly Cochrane whispered an order: 'Way enough. There's something dead ahead. I can't make it out yet.' The boat drifted slowly forward under its own momentum with the tide.

Then, 'Hold her, lads,' he said. 'Just look what we've got here!'

Dead in front of them, heaving slightly in the swell, was a mass of spars and tubs, weighted with stones and firmly moored by what, later, were revealed as five-and-a-quarter-ton anchors and outsize cables. It was a boom. It stretched right across that part of the channel in which the French fleet was moored. No ship could pass to the south of it because of the shoals; any ship trying to pass to the north would come into point-blank range of new batteries on the shore. No ship, it seemed, could possibly break straight through.

Allemand had disregarded Napoleon's views, and had taken additional precautions on his own account. Cochrane whistled quietly to himself and told his men to row back to the *Impérieuse*.

Next day, when the French admiral looked seawards, he realized that something unusual was going on, for Gambier's fleet was anchored eight miles off Aix in reasonably clear view, and was being augmented by what Allemand could plainly see were fireships.

'H'm,' he said. 'Fireships won't get through my boom. Still, I'd better take precautions.'

He ordered the ships to increase the distance between each to 170 yards, and to stow away all material, such as sails, which could easily be set on fire. Next he posted still more frigates in front of his lines, and collected seventy-three small boats which were to patrol continuously, night and day, just inside the boom. Then, as a demonstration of his sense of security, and as a gesture of contempt, he hung out a British ensign upside down from the heads (lavatories) of his flagship. He had reckoned with everything, he thought. Everything except Cochrane.

Cochrane had known nothing about the boom until he found it himself in the dark. Gambier had obviously not reconnoitred at all, which was just as well, for if he had known of the boom the idea of an attack would have been strangled at birth. But though he had known nothing of it, Cochrane already had in mind a weapon which was just the thing for dealing with it.

This secret weapon, with which he now decided to smash the boom, had never been used before. He called it an explosion vessel. It had the effect of a gigantic torpedo. It was to be used again a hundred years later in the first world war by Captain Campbell, V.C., in his attack on Zeebrugge, and later still by Captain Ryder, V.C., in his attack in the second world war at St. Nazaire.

Cochrane got together three old ships and, in his own words, prepared each one of them as follows:

'The floor of the vessel was rendered as firm as possible by means of racks placed in close contact, into every crevice of which other substances were firmly wedged so as to afford the greatest amount of resistance to the explosion. On this foundation were placed a large number of spirit and water casks, into which fifteen hundred barrels of powder were emptied. These casks were set on end, and the whole bound round with hempen cables so as to resemble a gigantic mortar, this causing the explosion to take an upward course. In addition to the powder casks were placed several hundred shells, and over these again nearly three thousand hand-grenades; the whole by means of wedges and sand being compressed as nearly as possible into a solid mass.'

While he himself was supervising the preparation of the torpedo ships, other officers were preparing twenty-three fireships. These ships were filled with all kinds of material which would burn easily, such as tarred canvas and shavings, and trains of quick-match were laid in troughs which ran fore and aft between decks. Up in the yard-arms masses of rockets devised by Mr. Congreve were fixed. In addition, four holes were cut in the main deck of each ship and ropes of well-tarred, twisted oakum were laid through these ports to the rigging and thence to the mastheads, so that the fires, once started below decks, would strike immediately to the topmost parts of the ship.

Cochrane, with two officers and four other men, decided to take charge personally of the first explosion ship. He would lead the way to the boom, followed by the second explosion ship. When he had lit the time fuses he would pull away in the ship's boat to the *Impérieuse*, leaving the torpedo ship to explode when the fuses had burned out. He would then come back again with the third explosion ship, which was to be moored temporarily to the *Impérieuse*. The three explosions would destroy the boom, he was sure, and the twenty-three fireships could then be loosed upon the enemy.

* * *

Cochrane had joined the fleet on April 3rd. Reconnoitring, discussion of plans, the preparation of fireships, and, above all, the construction of the explosion ships, had taken some days. Now, on April 11th, everything was ready. It looked as though conditions that night would be perfect. The tide was right, flowing strongly up the river. It would be a moonless, pitch-dark night, so that the French would see no movement until the torpedo ships were almost at the boom. The wind looked as though it would be right too, blowing hard in from the sea. Both torpedo ships and fireships would drive down before it at great speed. Cochrane got Gambier's permission to launch the attack that night.

Late in the afternoon, Cochrane in the *Impérieuse*, accompanied by three frigates and towing the explosion vessels, left the main fleet and moved cautiously towards the roads and the extreme edge of the Boyart shoal, farthest away from the Aix batteries. Then he set stern anchors, three miles from the boom and the French fleet, and waited.

Meanwhile, the officers who were to command the fire-ships went to the flagship for their last instructions, and then rowed away to take up their commands.

Even though it was still daylight, little if anything of these movements could be seen by the French, because visibility was so bad. Further, the wind had reached gale force, and the French guard-boats, which were supposed to be patrolling just inside the boom, were driven away from it by wind and tide, until they could see nothing but their own ships. Allemand had therefore no warning that an attack was proposed that night. He lay behind his boom, with no other fear than that one of his ships might drag her anchors.

Cochrane and his men also waited in their planned positions, knowing exactly what each had to do when the time came.

Night fell. The wind howled in the rigging. Waves smashed against the sterns of the ships.

Shortly before nine, Cochrane sent two small ships with lights to mark the extreme limit of the channel farthest away from the batteries. Because of mist and spray, the lights were invisible to any watchers on shore, but they would be seen by a ship which came close. Then, very silently, with his six volunteers, he boarded the explosion ship and cut loose, towing behind him the gig which was to be their one hope of safe return.

At once the ship, driven on by the wind and the tide, began to tear down the channel. Some distance from him the second torpedo ship also cut loose. Because the night was so dark that no one could see or be seen, this ship actually crashed into the boom before its crew knew where they were. Cochrane, however, managed to approach more gingerly.

'We're nearly on her. Heave to!'

Down came the tiny sail, and Cochrane swung the helm over to bring the ship broadside on to the boom, where she was held by the onrushing tide.

'Into the gig, lads, and stand by to cut the painter!'

While the tide swirled about them, and the spray hit their faces, the six men did what they could to hold the gig head on to the sea with her stern jammed against the side of the explosion vessel, waiting for Cochrane to follow them down. Cochrane took one last quick look round, then lit the fuses, and once he was sure they had caught he climbed over the side.

'Row for your lives, lads!'

It was easier said than done. The wind and tide had been allies going in, but now they were deadly enemies. It was hard to make any headway at all. But the seconds were ticking away, and already the fuses were hissing and spurting across the margin between black silence and sudden brilliant explosion.

Cochrane sat at the tiller looking back through the darkness at the hulk of his torpedo vessel. Suddenly, 'Good God!' he exclaimed. 'However did that get aboard?'

There on the deck of the explosion ship was a small dog, barking at the waves. If a patrol boat happened to be near and heard the barks, the crew would investigate. They might even put out the fuses.

Cochrane turned about, dashed back with the tide, and scooped the dog into the gig.

'Now, lads, we've lost two minutes. Only thirteen minutes to go. ROW!'

The men needed no order. They rowed.

The torpedo ship disappeared in the darkness, but their eyes could not leave the point where they had last seen its dimmed outline. One minute gone . . . two minutes . . . three minutes out of thirteen. Despite the gale and the cold spray, sweat was starting from their foreheads.

Four minutes . . . five minutes . . . how far away were they now? No one could tell. . . . They only knew that the fuses were burning through. Or were they? Cochrane had a sudden nightmare that somehow the spray or a wave washing over had put the fuses out. There would be no explosion at all, no blinding flash, to show that they had begun their work well and truly. Well, it was too late to turn back now.

Six minutes . . . nearly half the fuse should be gone by now, and the gig was nowhere near out of range yet.

'Pull, lads!'

The little boat tossed in the waves, spray spurting from its stern. But was it gaining on the tide? Or slipping back?

Seven minutes. . . . Then it happened. At one moment it was dark and the roar of gale and rushing water drowned all other sound. Next moment there was a terrific flash, followed by so great a detonation that the elemental roars themselves seemed silenced. The fuses had burned through in half the expected time.

Involuntarily the men in the gig stopped rowing, and bent their heads for safety. But quickly Cochrane looked back.

'For a moment,' he said, 'the sky was red with the lurid glare rising from the simultaneous ignition of fifteen hundred barrels of powder. On this gigantic flash subsiding, the air seemed alive with shells, grenades, rockets and masses of timber, the wreck of the vessel, whilst the water was strewn with spars shaken out of the enormous boom. . . . The sea was convulsed as by an earthquake, rising in a huge wave, on whose crest our boat was lifted like a cork and as suddenly dropped into a vast trough, out of which, as it closed on us with a rush of a whirlpool, none expected to emerge. The skill of the boat's crew, however, overcame the threatened danger, which passed away as suddenly as it had arisen.'

Because of the strong tide against them, and the loss of time caused by the dog, the gig was only a hundred yards away from the explosion. The bursting grenades and debris were flying over their heads and far beyond. Had they not gone back for the dog they would almost certainly have been killed by the lumps of metal and timber which crashed down from the skies into the sea.

After the huge wave had subsided, the seven men in the little gig pulled hard against the rolling sea in darkness and complete silence. Then suddenly, as one man, they yelled to each other. Another explosion lit the skies, clearly outlining the French fleet at anchor. It also clearly showed that where the boom had been a few minutes before, there was now nothing. The second explosion vessel, too, had done its work.

Still the men in the gig pulled away. In a few minutes there was a new and heartening sight, for to larboard, with flames pouring through the open ports and leaping to the rigging, came the first of the fireships, dead on course. Cochrane and his men watched it pass them, watched it to where the boom had been, saw it pass through unchecked, saw it head on for the French fleet. They knew then that they had succeeded. The way was open for the attack.

Almost immediately there came the sound of heavy firing. For a minute or two the French line-of-battle ships had been paralysed by the enormity of the explosion, but now as they saw the blazing fireship coming towards them they stood to their guns and blazed away. Unfortunately for them, they succeeded in hitting only their own frigates which had been placed ahead of them as protection. These frigates at once cut their cables, and, drifting between the French line-of-battle ships, added to the confusion which was now convulsing the roads.

Some of the fireships were badly managed. Some were lit too soon and burned out before they reached the French ships. Others were set on a wrong tack, so that they drifted uselessly on to shoals. One came so close to the *Impérieuse* that the acting captain ordered the torpedo vessel which was waiting alongside for Cochrane's return to be cut loose for fear she might be exploded by the errant fireship. In fact, only four out of twenty-three fireships actually reached the enemy, and although one of them became locked for a time with a French line-of-battle ship, none of them did any direct damage. But they caused utter chaos, because the French, having seen two ships explode violently, assumed that the oncoming fireships were explosion vessels too. They were not going to risk waiting until one of these ships exploded close by them. Nor were they going to set their sails and risk catching fire. So they simply cut their cables and, in the gale and fast-flooding tide, were quickly driven aground on one of the many shoals which lined the channel.

Six miles away the men in Gambier's fleet lined their ships to watch a display of fireworks such as no man had seen before. They saw the vast explosions of the torpedo ships. They saw the blazing fireships careering madly about the roads, their rockets spurting in all directions and their flames being torn upward by the gale. They saw for a time the

French guns firing into the night, and as the flashes lit up the sky they saw the huge French line-of-battle ships out of control, being driven helplessly to the shoals. They saw all this. They watched. But they did nothing. Lord Gambier, the commander-in-chief, was on his knees.

Two hours later streaks of light began to show in the eastern sky, and Cochrane, standing in the prow of the *Impérieuse*, could see the havoc he had caused. Thirteen French ships lay aground, and now that the tide was falling their sides were fast in the mud and their bottoms were exposed to the shot of any British ship that cared to approach them. They would remain thus helpless for some hours, until the tide flowed again.

As soon as it was light enough, Cochrane ran up his signal flags, so that the commander-in-chief, now nearly ten miles away, could know that he had the French fleet at his mercy. His first signal, at 5.48 a.m., read: 'Half the fleet can destroy the enemy. Seven on shore.' Gambier, getting up from his knees, merely hoisted the answering pennant, which is the equivalent in civilian life of sending a letter: 'Dear Sir, I have received your message. Yours truly . . .'

At 6.40 a.m., seeing through his glass that the fleet was making no move, Cochrane sent a second signal. It said: 'Eleven on shore.' Still Gambier replied only with the answering pennant.

An hour later, at 7.40 a.m., Cochrane sent a third signal saying: 'Only two afloat.' There was still only the answering pennant from Gambier.

Cochrane, exhausted from the night's efforts, paced his ship in mounting fury, every now and again putting his glass at the helpless French ships and then swinging round to put it on the unhelpful British fleet. There was no move from either. Flinging any remaining prudence to the wind, he ran up the contemptuous signal: 'The frigates alone can destroy the enemy.'

Then, nearly two hours later, at 9.30 a.m., he sent a signal from which despair, anger and contempt had for once removed all epithet. It simply stated: 'Enemy preparing to heave off.'

The tide was beginning to flow again. In an hour or two the French ships, now helpless on their sides, would be upright again, afloat, and, if necessary, able to fire. Still Gambier did not move. He did not trust Cochrane's soundings in the channel, least of all before the tide was full. He waited until eleven o'clock, and then at last Cochrane, black in the face from anger as well as dirt, saw that the fleet was weighing anchor.

It was still not too late. The tide once again was flowing fast. Most of the enemy ships were upright and a few were afloat, but none seemed yet in any condition for a fight. The British fleet moved nearer. But then, to Cochrane's amazement and fury, after half an hour it suddenly anchored again three miles from Aix and six miles from the nearest enemy ship. Only a few small ships were allowed to keep under way and come to reinforce Cochrane.

This was too much. From where he stood, Cochrane could see the French ships preparing to heave themselves off as the tide rose. He decided that, whatever Gambier might fail to do, he himself would go in to attack on his own. It was an extraordinarily brave thing to do, for in his comparatively small frigate he would have to face not only the shore batteries, such as they were, but also the full broadsides of those line-of-battle ships which were now getting afloat again. But he was probably too angry to think about the risks. He weighed anchor and let the *Impérieuse* drift stern foremost with the tide to the attack. He did not dare to make sail in case Gambier should see this and give him a direct order to return.

Upstream he went with the tide, and then, suddenly making sail after the first French ship to get off the shoal, he sent a new signal to Gambier, saying: 'Enemy superior to chasing ship but inferior to the fleet.' As this signal produced no reaction except the now monotonous answering pennant, he decided to force Gambier's hand by signalling: 'In want of assistance.' He then proceeded to fire on the *Calcutta*, a British ship of fourteen guns, which had been captured by the French and was now being used as an ammunition store. Simultaneously he fired with his fo'c'sle and bow guns on two seventy-fours which were still aground close by. His fire on the *Calcutta* was so effective that the French captain, believing that his ship would shortly explode, led his crew into the boats and pulled away. For this act he was subsequently court-martialled and shot. Meanwhile other ships succeeded in heaving off, and some of them, throwing their guns overboard to lighten themselves, made off as fast as they could up-river.

At last, in answer to his signal demanding assistance, two line-of-battle ships and five frigates from the fleet came sailing up the roads and began to fire on those Frenchmen who were still aground. At five-thirty two of these struck their colours. At six the crew of the *Tornoise* set fire to her and abandoned ship, leaving her to blow up. At nine the abandoned *Calcutta* also blew up.

The action ceased at nightfall, but the men in the *Impérieuse* remained alert. At first light they saw what to them was a heartbreaking sight. Gambier had hoisted recall lights for

the ships which had come in to help Cochrane. These at
once weighed anchor, and as they passed the *Impérieuse*,
Cochrane, still without any sleep, filthy dirty and utterly
exhausted, stood at the side of his ship calling to them across
the water, begging them to stay. As they were bound to do,
the ships swung by in silence. Cochrane, four brigs and his
old ship the *Pallas* were left alone in the roads.

Cochrane was determined to remain. Although his men,
like himself, were sleepless, he set them to repair what
damage the *Impérieuse* had suffered. Throughout the fighting
only three men had been killed and a few wounded, but
enemy shot had pierced the sides of the ship and had
damaged the foremast. While still at work on the repairs, as
the light strengthened he looked towards the *Caledonia*, and
saw that Gambier had at last hoisted a signal which was not
the answering pennant. It was the recall signal. Cochrane at
once replied: 'If permitted to remain can destroy the
enemy.' There was no immediate reply to this, but after a
time a boat came alongside with a letter from Gambier
telling Cochrane (*a*) that he had done well, (*b*) that he must
return at once, (*c*) that if he really thought fit he could
attack ships which were still aground. Ignoring the fact that
this message was completely contradictory, Cochrane merely
replied that he could destroy the ships which were still
aground; and indeed as he sent the message over the side
he could see the French still throwing guns overboard and
loading their stores into small boats to lighten the ships.

He was now ready for the attack. But just as he was preparing
to weigh anchor he received a further message from Gambier
telling him that an officer was being sent to relieve him and
that he himself must return to the *Caledonia* at once. He still
did not give up. On board the *Caledonia* he continued to

press Gambier to drive into the roads and destroy what remained of the enemy. Gambier's reply was that he must finish his dispatches and send them off to England.

Cochrane was a daredevil captain in charge of a few ships, whose loss would not have affected the outcome of the war. Gambier was in charge of the whole fleet, whose loss would have been disastrous. Even so, it seemed to Cochrane then, and has seemed to historians since, that Gambier's caution amounted to dereliction of duty.

Years later, Cochrane was told of an event which, if he had known about it at the time, would have made him ruder to Gambier on the quarterdeck of the *Caledonia* than Admiral Harvey had been. It appears that a French quartermaster hid himself on board the *Ocean*, a line-of-battle ship which had been deserted by the rest of her crew when she grounded. Some time later a British midshipman of seventeen was sent in a jolly-boat with a message to another ship. Instead of returning to his own ship as soon as he had delivered the message, he suggested to his men that they should close one of the grounded French ships just for fun. In the darkness they came alongside the three-decker *Ocean*, and thought of boarding her. But they were challenged. The hidden quartermaster shouted '*Qui vive?*' and made the little midshipman and his handful of a boat's crew believe that the *Ocean* was still manned. So they stood off.

If he had known the truth, he and his crew of four could have taken immediate possession of a three-decker and two deserted seventy-fours which lay alongside her. If a midshipman and four men could have done that, there is little doubt that Gambier and his ships could have destroyed every ship in the French fleet, probably without loss to themselves. Gambier, however, did not think it prudent to come nearer than six miles from the nearest French ship, or to allow men who were on the spot to complete the action they had so brilliantly begun.

As it was, with all the restrictions placed upon him, and Gambier's refusal of co-operation, Cochrane had succeeded in the task he had been set. The French squadron never again left the Aix Roads. Allemand was disgraced, and the admiral who succeeded him merely fitted up what remained of his ships as blocks to ward off any new attack. From then until Napoleon's final defeat the British at sea were freed from any further French threat. The last French strongholds in the West Indies were scooped up without a shot being fired, and our trade across the Atlantic went forward peacefully.

Cochrane, however, did not go forward peacefully. Gambier ordered him to England with dispatches, and there he was hailed as a popular hero. Broadsheets, those nineteenth-century English equivalent of the modern West Indian calypsos, were full of his name. Bonfires were lit on hill-tops. Special medals were made, and Cochrane himself was created a Knight of the Order of the Bath.

But inwardly he was fuming, and when he heard that it was proposed to move a vote of thanks in the House of Commons to Lord Gambier for his services, he wrote to the Admiralty to say that if any such motion appeared on the order paper he would oppose it. The First Sea Lord not merely begged him to refrain, but offered him at once something which he had always wanted, the independent command not just of one ship but of a whole squadron, with the right, under independent orders, to harry the French and Spanish coasts at will. Cochrane rejected the offer.

He could not forgive Gambier for falling so far short of

Nelson's advice to go straight at 'em. When Gambier heard what Cochrane meant to do, he himself demanded a court martial, and the Tory Government of the day saw to it that the court was packed with Gambier's friends and Cochrane's enemies. The president was Sir Roger Curtis, who was a lifelong friend of Gambier, and the senior admiral on the board was none other than the same Sir William Young who had demanded half of Cochrane's prize money in the *Pallas* days, and had several times been attacked by Cochrane in the House of Commons for incompetence.

Gambier was acquitted. Then, for what he had done, which actively was nothing, he was given a vote of thanks by Parliament. Cochrane, who single-handed had devised and who almost single-handed had executed the plan whereby the last great threat of Napoleon's fleet was finally removed from the seas, was never again in his lifetime placed in command of a British ship at war.

6. The Stock Exchange Mystery

THE ATTACKS which Cochrane had made on Lord Gambier damned him with Admiralty. The attacks which he continued to make on Lord Liverpool damned him with the Government. He was offered no command of any sort during the next three and a half years. He busied himself with inventions and with exposing scandals in the Admiralty Prize Court in Malta. But he was soon to be involved in a scandal of his own which brought him humiliation and disaster.

At the beginning of 1814 he had at long last received a new naval appointment—flag captain to his uncle, Sir Alexander Cochrane, who had recently been made commander-in-chief on the North American Station. The fleet out there was in poor shape after the rough handling it had received from the Americans in the war of 1812, and Sir Alexander sailed at once to see what he could do to put things right. Cochrane was left behind to supervise the fitting out of the flagship, the *Tonnant*, at Chatham, with instructions to put to sea in her as soon as he could. He never put to sea in her.

Late at night on February 20th, a stranger in the scarlet

uniform of a French royalist regiment and with a white cockade in his hat arrived at an inn in Dover, saying that he had just come from France.

'Napoleon has been killed! The allied sovereigns are now in Paris!' he shouted to the landlord.

Then, sending off his news by messenger to the Port Admiral, he jumped into a coach and left for London.

Wherever he stopped along the route he spread the good news, and in his delight tipped lavishly with golden French louis at every halt. But the coachman noticed that when they drew into London itself his passenger pulled up the blinds of his coach and travelled the remainder of the way inconspicuously until he reached Lambeth. There he jumped out, hastily paid off the coachman, and, disregarding the fact that its driver was obviously drunk, he hired a hackney, and in it disappeared for a time from view.

His news had travelled almost as fast as he did, and had grown as it travelled. Within an hour the Stock Exchange had heard not only that Napoleon was defeated but that a party of French royalists was even now driving into the City and shouting '*Vive le Roi!*' to all the bystanders.

At once there was a scramble to buy. Stock and share prices, which for some weeks had been depressed, shot skywards. Omnium, which four days before had stood at 17, opened at 27½ and reached 32 in the afternoon. Other prices followed this lead.

But by late afternoon the rumours were dying down. The British Government knew nothing of Napoleon's alleged defeat. The private banking houses had heard nothing from their Continental agents. The Stock Exchange began to feel that it had been hoaxed. There was a wave of selling.

Omnium slumped back to 26½, a point below its opening price.

When on the following day the 'defeat' was officially denied by the Government, the Committee of the Stock Exchange began to make inquiries.

They looked through the bargains made on February 21st. Had anyone made heavy profits that day by selling stocks during the few hours of the boom? The Committee found seven names. Among them were Andrew Cochrane Johnstone, M.P., one of Cochrane's uncles, Richard Gathorne Butt, Cochrane's stockbroker, and—Cochrane himself.

On March 7th the Stock Exchange offered a reward of £250 for the arrest of the scarlet-uniformed officer who had first spread the false rumour. All they knew about him was that he had signed himself 'Du Bourg' in his letter to the Port Admiral at Dover, and that he had disappeared at Lambeth. They were soon to hear a rumour, however, that when Du Bourg had paid off his coach and taken the hackney carriage, he had driven directly to the house of Lord Cochrane.

Because of his own heavy sales of stock on the day of the hoax, because even larger sales on their own behalf were made by his uncle and his stockbroker, and because Du Bourg, the originator of the hoax, seemed to have gone straight to him on arrival in London, things looked black for Cochrane. Wasn't it, anyway, just the sort of trick that fellow would delight in playing?

On March 8th Cochrane seemed to paint himself blacker still. He admitted publicly that Du Bourg had, in fact, come to his house, that he had known Du Bourg personally for some time under the name of Charles Random de Berenger, that on the day in question he had given this de Berenger a change of clothes. A change of clothes? Whatever for? Obviously, having done his part of the job, de Berenger wanted to hide his conspicuous French uniform and escape in something less showy—and Cochrane had aided and abetted him.

Some three days later a scarlet uniform was found in the Thames and was identified by a London tailor as one which he had sold to de Berenger on February 17th.

For a time nothing more happened. Cochrane stayed down at Chatham, preparing the flagship for sea, ignoring the rumours and accusations which were now freely circulating. Then four weeks later de Berenger himself was arrested in Scotland trying to ship himself abroad in disguise. Two weeks later still, on April 20th, after de Berenger had been closely questioned, Cochrane, his uncle, his stockbroker, four others and de Berenger himself were formally charged with unlawfully conspiring to defraud investors and make a profit for themselves by spreading false news.

Cochrane could no longer stand aloof. His friends insisted that he should make some public statement, and under their pressure he went to his lawyer and swore an affidavit.

He said that on the morning of the hoax he had gone into the City to spend some hours with a manufacturer who was making the Cochrane convoy lamp. While he was with the manufacturer, a messenger came from his house to say that an officer was asking to see him urgently. He was, in fact, expecting a messenger from Spain, where his brother was gravely ill. He finished his business with the manufacturer, and went home. There he found, not the officer he had been expecting, but de Berenger.

He had met this man socially on several occasions, and had talked to him professionally. De Berenger, like Cochrane himself, was something of a chemist, and had experimented with explosives. More important still, he was an expert sharp-shooter. Because in North America there was likely to be a good deal of sniping at British ships when they lay close inshore, Sir Alexander Cochrane had asked Admiralty to appoint de Berenger as sharpshooting instructor on the North American Station. Admiralty had refused, but de Berenger had tried to persuade Cochrane none the less to take him aboard the *Tonnant*.

'That,' said Cochrane, 'was all I knew of de Berenger until he arrived at my house on the morning of February 21st.'

When he got home that morning, Cochrane continued, de Berenger again asked for at least a passage in the *Tonnant*, though he now pleaded debts and not sharpshooting as his reason for the voyage. He was, he said, being seriously pressed by creditors. He was already in a debtors' prison, and was only at large that day because debtors were allowed out provided they did not go more than a certain distance from the prison. He now wanted to take advantage of this rule and escape from the country.

'You know I can't do what you ask without Admiralty permission,' said Cochrane.

'Well, My Lord, at least do one thing for me. When I left prison this morning I went home and changed into this uniform. I thought that perhaps you would take me straight away as a sharpshooter, and I wanted to be properly dressed to go aboard the *Tonnant*.'

Cochrane looked at the uniform. It was, he said in his affidavit, not the scarlet of the French royalists, but the green of the sharpshooters.

'If I have to go back to the prison like this,' de Berenger went on, 'the authorities will know that I have broken bounds.

My house is well outside the rules. Will you please lend me a cloak and hat to cover the uniform? I'll then be able to get back undetected and change into ordinary clothes when I'm inside.'

Cochrane was packing for his own voyage. Coats and suits lay about his rooms. He handed over an old coat and hat. De Berenger put these on, stuffed his sharpshooter's overcoat and hat into the portmanteau he was carrying, and left.

Such was Cochrane's affidavit. Much of it could be proved true. De Berenger *was* an expert sharpshooter. Sir Alexander Cochrane *had* asked Admiralty permission to take him to North America. Cochrane *had* met him socially at his uncle's house, and *had* discussed sharpshooting and pyrotechnics with him. But there was a big doubt in his story. Every witness who could be found who had seen de Berenger masquerading as Du Bourg stated that he was wearing a scarlet uniform. Cochrane swore then, and continued to swear until his dying day, that when de Berenger was at his house he was wearing green.

The point was vitally important. If de Berenger really had been wearing green, there was no reason for Cochrane to be suspicious of him, or why he should not have lent him a coat when he heard the story of the debtors' prison. But if, in fact, de Berenger was wearing French scarlet, Cochrane could not fail to have been suspicious.

Something of which there was no doubt whatever, however, was that Cochrane had sold £139,000 worth of Omnium stock on the morning of the hoax. He said he had bought this holding out of his prize money late in the previous year, when it looked as though Napoleon would be quickly defeated. He had appointed Mr. Butt as his stockbroker because, as a one-time clerk in Portsmouth dockyard, Butt had naval connections. Cochrane had given Butt instructions to sell this holding if ever it rose one point above the price at which he bought it. On the morning of the hoax, the moment the one-point limit was reached, Butt had duly sold out, though he himself and Cochrane Johnstone had waited until later in the day, when the increase was much more than one point, before they sold their own holdings.

Cochrane seemed convinced that these explanations would be readily accepted. He did not even bother to read the brief his counsel had prepared. He went on as before, getting the *Tonnant* ready for sea. This was a disastrous mistake, typical of Cochrane when only his own interests were at risk.

True, the *Tonnant* was important; true, he was certain of his own innocence. But couldn't he see that the prima facie case against him was serious? Even if he was blind to that, didn't he realize that both Government and Admiralty would do him down if they could? Wasn't he right up against the 'establishment'? Hadn't he suspected political trickery even when he was asked to lead the attack on Aix Roads? His friends crowded round him impatiently.

'For God's sake do something! This is serious.'

Cochrane did something. He went on preparing the *Tonnant* for sea.

While Cochrane worked on his ship, the prosecution worked on Cochrane. The official complainants were the Committee of the Stock Exchange. But instead of using their own solicitors, the Committee appointed—or were induced to appoint—a Mr. Lavie to act for them. Cochrane knew all about Mr. Lavie. Mr. Lavie was solicitor to the Admiralty. He had been the man behind the defence at Gambier's court martial and one of Cochrane's most bitter opponents. His appointment to prepare the Stock Exchange case should

have warned Cochrane that other interests more powerful
than the Stock Exchange were now at work against him.

Soon another warning light had begun to blink. When,
under pressure of his friends, he had at last agreed to make a
public statement, Cochrane had sworn his affidavit before a
Mr. Gurney, one of the leading counsel of the day. Before
swearing his affidavit, he had thoroughly discussed his case
with Mr. Gurney. He now heard that Mr. Gurney, after
accepting his confidences, had also accepted the job of
leading the prosecution against him.

Then came the worst blow of all. The Lord Chief Justice,
Lord Ellenborough, announced that he himself would preside
at the trial. Lord Ellenborough was not only Lord Chief
Justice. He was also an ex-Cabinet Minister of a party with
which Cochrane was in continuous and bitter parliamentary
conflict. Of all the Tories he was the most reactionary. Only
recently, with a relish which he did not try to conceal, he
had sent Cochrane's political and personal friend Cobbett to
prison for a year for writing an anti-Government pamphlet
and had fined him £1,000. Did he now see the chance to
get rid of another political trouble-maker?

The danger signals were there for all to see, but Cochrane
would not look. Even when the trial opened on June 8th,
1814, he obstinately refused to attend. That was his crowning
folly.

Mr. Gurney opened the case for the prosecution at 9 a.m.,
and at once made his tactics clear. There seemed to be little
doubt of the guilt of the other accused. Beyond dispute, de
Berenger had spread the rumour. Witness after witness was
brought to identify him. He was known to have been in the
pay of Cochrane Johnstone. Indeed, notes found on him
when he was arrested were traced back both to Cochrane

Johnstone and to Butt. Cochrane Johnstone's own record was bad. He had been court-martialled on a charge of dishonesty and cashiered from the Army. Subsequently he had made a fortune out of the slave trade, smuggling, corruption in the West Indies, where he had held a Government post, and particularly flagrant profiteering in the Peninsular War. He had lost some of this fortune gambling on the Stock Exchange, and was now heavily in debt.

Unlike Cochrane, neither Cochrane Johnstone nor Butt had long-standing general arrangements to sell their holdings on any small rise. Their operations on that fateful Monday had been carefully planned. They had spent the whole of the day in the City watching the market carefully, and only sold out in the late afternoon, when they judged that the rumours had had full effect and that prices were at their peak.

Mr. Gurney knew he would have no difficulty in securing the conviction of these two, of de Berenger and of others who were charged, but he was not so sure of Cochrane. So he turned all his fire on him. Mr. Scarlett, Cochrane's counsel, had seen that this would happen, and had begged Cochrane to demand a separate trial. Without the dead weight of the other accused, Cochrane, he thought, was certain of acquittal. But in dealings with his family, Cochrane had a strong sense of loyalty. His uncle might be a scoundrel, but he would not abandon him now. They would stand or fall together.

All morning, all afternoon, right on into the night the prosecution's witnesses were examined. The landlord at the Dover inn, the coachman, the drunken hackney driver, the Jewish tailor, ostlers, pot-boys, Stock Exchange officials, all followed each other in steady succession, until the courtroom grew stuffy and the jurors began to drowse in the hot June air. The case for the prosecution was not completed until

ten o'clock at night, and now, at last, counsel, jurors, witnesses and the judge himself would be able to stretch themselves and go home for a night's rest. Serjeant Best, who was
leading the defence for Cochrane Johnstone and Butt, at
once asked for an adjournment.

But Lord Ellenborough would not have it. The jury were
now so tired that they could not possibly take in further
argument, even if counsel were still fresh enough to present
it. But Lord Ellenborough persisted.

'Witnesses have been waiting throughout the day. They
can't attend tomorrow without great public inconvenience.
Pray proceed with your case, Serjeant Best. If necessary I
will sit right through the night.'

So, at 10 p.m., after thirteen hours of almost continuous
session, Best opened his clients' case. Or rather, in the hope
that the probably innocent might save the certainly guilty, he
opened what amounted to Cochrane's case. Cochrane
Johnstone, Butt and the others had little defence; so little
was said about them. Cochrane had a strong defence; so much
was said about that. But on Cochrane's own instructions,
nothing was said on his behalf which might harm his uncle.

Through the night Serjeant Best struggled with his opening speech and then with the examination of his witnesses.
There were, he said, only two points which at all suggested
that Cochrane himself was concerned in the hoax. One was
that, admittedly, he had sold a large block of stock on the
Monday and so had made a considerable profit. But Serjeant
Best emphasized once again that these sales had taken place
under standing arrangements made as long ago as the previous
November. But many cautious investors, said Best, had such
arrangements. The prosecution had brought no evidence
whatever to suggest that there was anything unusual about

Cochrane's own arrangement. They did not suggest that Cochrane had given special orders to sell on the Monday. They did not even suggest that Cochrane had been near the Stock Exchange on that day, or that he had been in touch at all with his broker.

The second point against him was his meeting with de Berenger. Best went in detail through the affidavit which Cochrane had already sworn.

Turning to the jury, he asked: 'Do you really believe that if His Lordship had known about the hoax he would have allowed the man who has confessed to be the chief agent of the hoax to come openly to his house? If he had been unable to prevent de Berenger from coming to his house, do you still believe that he would have stayed talking with him openly for upwards of an hour? Would not a guilty man have sent de Berenger packing at once?'

Serjeant Best had made a strong case so far, though whether the weary jury were at all capable of taking it in was doubtful. He now came to the really difficult point about the uniform which de Berenger had worn while he was at Cochrane's house. There was no doubt that in the inn at Dover he had been wearing royalist scarlet. There was no doubt that he had still been wearing royalist scarlet during the stages of his journey to London. At Lambeth, when he left the coach, there were witnesses to swear that he was still wearing scarlet. Finally, Crane, the driver of the hackney carriage, swore that he was wearing scarlet when he entered Cochrane's house. But Cochrane in his affidavit swore that de Berenger was wearing the sharpshooter's green when he saw him.

In dealing with this conflict of evidence Serjeant Best was weak. It was not his fault that he was not able to call Cochrane and let him make his own explanations. Cochrane was not present. But it was his fault that he did not put some possibilities to the jury. It was known that during the approach to London, de Berenger had hidden himself behind the blinds of the coach. Perhaps he had changed then, and the coachman, tired after his journey, and busy collecting the fare, had not particularly noticed the change. Or again, de Berenger might have changed in the hackney. Witnesses agreed that the driver was drunk. Was he in any state to say what uniform his passenger was wearing? Finally, there was that interval between de Berenger's arrival at Cochrane's house and Cochrane's return from the City. He had time to change then and to stuff his scarlet into the portmanteau he was carrying.

All of these were possibilities which ought to have been put to the jury. Instead, Serjeant Best merely suggested that perhaps his client was mistaken. He had been used to seeing de Berenger in green, had taken no particular notice of what he was wearing, and perhaps had thought that he was still wearing green. This was, to say the least, an unlikely possibility. Lord Ellenborough was to make the most of it.

The case ground on until three o'clock in the morning, and by this time some of the jurors were literally asleep. All were exhausted. At last Ellenborough agreed to adjourn until 10 a.m. Then, through a second day, the jury tried to concentrate, while witnesses were cross-examined, counsel made their final speeches, and for three solid hours Lord Ellenborough summed up. The summing-up did not deal with one point in Cochrane's favour. Again and again Lord Ellenborough came back to that point of the uniform. The uniform, he said, was striking in colour. No one could mistake it. De Berenger had entered Cochrane's house dressed in it.

Cochrane must have seen him in it. If he had been innocent, he must have been suspicious. No innocent man seeing that uniform would have lent de Berenger a disguise.

At 6.10 p.m. the Lord Chief Justice had finished and the jury filed away to their room. Exactly two and a half hours later they came back to give their verdict on all the prisoners. Their verdict was 'Guilty'.

*   *   *

In those days an interval elapsed between verdict and sentence. During that interval, Cochrane Johnstone and another of the accused fled to the Continent. Butt followed them the moment sentence was pronounced.

Cochrane himself appeared in court six days later before Lord Ellenborough to ask for a new trial on the grounds that he wished to produce fresh evidence. Lord Ellenborough disposed of his plea with contumely in a few minutes, and six days later he came up for judgment, before another judge. He and his fellow defendants were sentenced to a year's imprisonment, an hour in the pillory outside the Royal Exchange, and a fine of £1,000.

There was immediate public uproar at the savagery of this sentence, and when Sir Francis Burdett, who now shared the representation of the Borough of Westminster with Cochrane in the House of Commons, announced that he would stand in the pillory beside Cochrane, the Government decided to remit this part of the sentence, and shortly afterwards abolished the pillory entirely. But the fine and imprisonment stood.

Cochrane was dismissed from the Navy; the banner which he flew as a Knight of the Order of the Bath was ceremonially kicked out of Westminster Abbey; he was expelled from the

House of Commons and lodged in the King's Bench. His constituency immediately re-elected him to the House, one of his old opponents, Sheridan the playwright, refusing to stand against him, and in pennies and sixpences collected more than enough to pay his fine.

Cochrane himself tried to get over the prison sentence by escaping from the King's Bench by means of a rope which he looped over some nearby railings. Despite a heavy fall he managed to make his way to his country home, and remained there unmolested for a week. Then he suddenly appeared in the House of Commons in the hope of being able to argue against imprisonment on the grounds of privilege, but as he had not taken the oath on his re-election he had no standing, and was forcibly returned to prison after a stand-up fight in the lobbies. There he remained.

He was still kept there after the full year had expired, because he refused to pay his fine or to allow anyone else to pay it for him. But at last, because his doctors told him that his health was seriously suffering from confinement, he paid the fine with a £1,000 note which is still preserved in the Bank of England. On it he wrote: 'My health having suffered by long and close confinement, and my oppressors being resolved to deprive me of property or life, I submit to robbery to protect myself from murder, in the hope that I shall live to bring the delinquents to justice.' This note was signed on July 3rd, 1815, just fifteen days after Wellington's victory at Waterloo.

*   *   *

At the time many leading lawyers were convinced that, if Cochrane had agreed to a separate trial and a separate defence, he would have been acquitted. Despite the damaging doubt about the uniform, three Lord Chancellors in turn declared that in their opinion he was innocent.

More convincing even than the opinion of Lord Chancellors, however, was some fresh evidence which came out long after Cochrane had finished his sentence. One was the word of a reliable witness who had seen de Berenger at Dover before he went flamboyantly into that inn. This witness declared that, when he saw him, de Berenger was wearing sharpshooter's green. This showed at least that he had that uniform with him. The second piece of evidence affected Crane, the hackney driver. Crane revealed to friends that on the day in question he had been so drunk that he had no idea how his fare was dressed. He said that, in fact, he had been offered money to say that the man was in scarlet. When this news reached the authorities, Crane was prosecuted for perjury and was convicted.

But perhaps the most revealing evidence of all that Cochrane was, in fact, innocent, came forty-five years later, when he was within a year of his death.

He had just published the first volume of his *Autobiography of a Seaman*, and one morning a few weeks later the postman brought him a letter. He did not recognize the handwriting. He opened the envelope and found that the writer was his first cousin, the daughter of his uncle Cochrane Johnstone. The letter read:

'You are still active, still in health, and you have just given to the world a striking proof of the vigour of your mind and intellect. Many years I cannot wish for you; but may you live to finish your book, and, if it pleases God, may you and I have a peaceful deathbed. We have both suffered mental anguish, though in various degrees; for yours was indeed the hardest lot that an honourable man can be called on to bear.

Oh, my dear cousin, let me say once more, whilst we are still here, how, ever since that miserable time, I have felt that you have suffered for my poor father's fault—how agonizing that conviction was—how thankful I am that tardy justice was done you. May God return you four-fold for your generous though misplaced confidence in him and for all your subsequent forbearance.'

None of these expressions of view after the event, however, helped Cochrane. He was dismissed from the service he loved and in which he had been outstandingly successful; and in the eyes of many people he was for a time dishonoured. Neither the dismissal nor the dishonour remained.

7. Against the Odds

Sparks from the French Revolution fell on almost every country in the world. In England they quickly set Charles James Fox ablaze and, though his fire died, some of its embers continued to smoulder in such men as Place, Sir Francis Burdett—and Cochrane. Far away in South America a whole continent burst into flames. But there, as Cochrane was to find, the revolution was an excuse for adventurers almost as much as it was an opportunity for idealists.

For years Spain and Portugal between them had dominated South America, plundering its enormous accumulations of gold and silver, oppressing the native Indian races with unexampled cruelty, and ruling with a tight hand even their own fellow countrymen who had settled there. So, in Chile, Peru, Brazil and elsewhere, liberal-minded men who resented tyranny strained at the yoke. For them the French Revolution was a beacon of freedom.

But the riches of South America had attracted not only the far-off governments in Madrid and Lisbon but also adventurers from all over the world. Such men cared nothing for ideas of freedom and equality. They wanted to break the power of Spain and Portugal only because they wanted power for themselves. To them freedom meant only keeping for themselves the riches which hitherto had drained away across the sea.

Besides these two groups there were the loyalists of the Spanish and Portuguese establishments—the military and naval garrisons and the civil servants—who were satisfied with their share of the pickings under the imperial governments, and the Indians, who saw in civil war the only hope of retrieving a position for themselves, and were ready at all times to attack either side.

So, even when the revolts which the French Revolution had inspired were successful, the rebels almost invariably quarrelled among themselves, and the imperial powers, sending reinforcements from Europe, had been able to re-establish themselves at least in part. Although the revolts had been almost continuous since 1794, twenty-five years later the whole of Peru, three northern provinces of Brazil and one province of Chile were still possessed by either Spain or Portugal.

It was into this medley of incompatibles that, full of political idealism, which was not yet acceptable even in his own country, Cochrane plunged in November 1818.

Cochrane had served his year in prison and had returned to the House of Commons, but by now the Napoleonic wars were over, and, in any event, he was ostracized by his beloved Royal Navy. His main consolations now were his wife and two young children.

His marriage had itself been as romantic as his naval career. He had met a young orphan girl from the Midlands called Katharine Barnes. She was very lovely. Cochrane fell in love with her at once and soon they were secretly engaged.

Rumours of this reached another of his uncles, Basil Cochrane, who had made a fortune in the East Indies, and was determined that Cochrane, either by a wealthy marriage or by some other means, should make a fortune too, and so restore the Dundonald family fortunes, which had been so finally dissipated by the ninth Earl and his inventions. Uncle Basil at once summoned Cochrane.

'My boy,' he said, 'it's time you were married, and I have found the right girl for you. She is the daughter of an Admiralty prize-court official. You know what that means. Her father has made a lot of money, and if you marry the girl it will all be yours.'

'Uncle, you know as well as I do that I have spent a number of years exposing the corruption in these courts. If I now marry into a family which has benefited from that corruption, no one will ever look at me again. My constituents in Westminster would hoot at me.'

Uncle Basil made a sharp comment on the voters in Westminster and in any other constituency. He told his nephew to think things over. Cochrane did. He went straight to Miss Barnes, persuaded her to fly with him to Scotland, and there they were married. Uncle Basil not only cut him out of his own will but sent word that he did not wish to see him again, or at least not often.

Despite the great and lasting happiness of his marriage, Cochrane still longed for the sea and for a more fruitful arena for his developing political views than was offered by an unreformed House of Commons. At last one day the chance came.

The Republic of Chile, determined to strengthen its frail independence by winning control of the South Pacific, instructed its envoy in London to find some outstanding seaman who would take over the command of the Chilean Navy, such as it was.

In February 1818 the envoy replied to his Government: 'I have extreme satisfaction in informing you that Lord Cochrane, one of the most eminent and valiant seamen of Great Britain, has undertaken to proceed to Chile to direct our navy. He is a person highly commendable, not only on account of the liberal principles with which he has always upheld the cause of the English people in their Parliament, but also because he bears a character altogether superior to ambitious self-seeking.'

Five months later Cochrane, his wife and children were on their way to Chile.

*   *   *

Two men, leading the Chilean patriot army, had driven the Spanish garrisons out of all Chile except for a single province. One of these men was San Martin, a man without formal education, but none the less a great soldier, remarkable for his great black beard and his cunning eyes. After the victory, and to the universal surprise, he did not appoint himself director of the new nominally independent state. Later he was to show that this 'modesty' was just a part of his usual cunning. But in the meantime he seemed satisfied that his deputy, O'Higgins, the weak, well-meaning, illegitimate son of an Irish immigrant, should have the job.

Both San Martin and O'Higgins knew that their victory was precarious. Though the Spaniards had been driven almost completely from the land, they still commanded the seas. At any moment they might bring an expeditionary force either from Spain or from neighbouring Peru, which

they still strongly held, and recover their lost Chilean terri-
tories. Almost as bad, they were in a position to blockade the
Chilean patriots by sea. At that stage of South American
development this was a serious matter. Chile, like its neighbours, had few roads. Travellers into the interior had to go
on horseback along narrow tracks, through forests alive with
savage and resentful Indians. The defiles through the
mountains sometimes ran along the edge of precipices, and
were so narrow that there was room only for a single rider,
so that if two horsemen met head on, one had to turn round
and retire. Lady Cochrane herself once came face to face
with a Chilean royalist brandishing a pistol, but her servant
edged past her and sent the royalist scampering back the
way he had come.

The countryside was interrupted with torrents which
roared through deep ravines and could only be crossed in
single file by rope bridges which swayed frighteningly in the
slightest wind. Lady Cochrane had another adventure on one
of these. She had taken her son on a visit to some friends
inland, when the boy was taken ill. With a personal fear-
lessness which equalled her husband's, she decided to rush
the boy back to a doctor on the coast. But just as she reached
one of these bridges she saw a band of royalists chasing her.
Without hesitation, she picked up her son from the stretcher
on which he was being carried, told her servants to scatter
in the forest, and herself dashed on to the bridge, clutching
the boy in her arms. The speed at which she ran, and the
force of the wind, set the bridge swaying so violently that
she felt she would lose her balance at any moment. To stop
the swaying, she lay down with her son in the very centre of
the bridge, while the torrent roared beneath her, and the
shouts and pistol shots of the royalist pursuers came closer

and closer. As the swaying diminished, one of her servants came after her, picked the boy from her arms, and completed the crossing to the other side, with Lady Cochrane following behind him. Then he cut the ropes of the bridge, which plunged into the ravine, taking some of the royalists with it.

Such primitive means of communication as these in the interior forced the Chilenos to travel and to supply themselves by ships which traded along their immense coastline. But the sea was now denied them. Cochrane's job was to remedy this.

*   *   *

When he reached Valparaiso, the Chilean Navy consisted of one sixty-four-gun ship, one forty-four-gun ship, and four small brigs of sixteen to eighteen guns, apart from a flagship which was a forty-eight-gun frigate recently captured from the Spanish and renamed the *O'Higgins*. To man all these ships there were a number of foreign officers, but no more than two hundred men, not all of whom had even been to sea before.

Among the foreign officers was the British Major Miller, who was in command of the marines, and became Cochrane's firm friend. But two other Britons, Guys and Spry, both of whom were called captain only by courtesy of the Chilenos, were brave but wholly unscrupulous buccaneers, who thought that the appointment of Cochrane might interfere with their buccaneering, and who spent most of their time intriguing for his dismissal with the equally corrupt Minister of Marine, Zenteno.

But Cochrane did have some assets. General O'Higgins steadily supported him, except when he asked for pay for himself or his seamen. The Chilean Admiral Blanco Encelada, whom he had been brought out to supersede, gave him absolute loyalty. The great mass of ordinary Chilean people, who had heard of his exploits off the Spanish coast and in the Mediterranean, looked on him as a god. In this they differed from the Spaniards in Peru and in the one still-occupied Chilean province. These too had heard of Cochrane's exploits and referred to him as El Diablo.

Cochrane's career with the Chilean Navy began disconcertingly. He had sighted some Spanish ships offshore, and at once put out to meet them. But just as his flagship was weighing anchor, he saw his five-year-old son being carried on board from one of the ship's boats. The boy had run away from his mother, determined to see his father fight. Cochrane locked him in his cabin and went about his duties. He was soon within range of the enemy and opened fire. But taking his eyes for a moment from the battle, he looked towards one of his main-deck guns. There, standing upright and unperturbed among the gun's crew, was his son, who had crawled from the cabin through an air-vent and had come on deck. Before the father could move or shout, an enemy shot struck and killed a marine who was standing beside his son. The boy was spattered with blood, but, still unperturbed, he came running to his father and cried: 'Jack says that the ball is not yet made which can hurt Tommy.' Cochrane let him stay on deck for the rest of the action.

This, however, did not last long, because other ships which had accompanied the flagship to sea almost at once refused to obey orders. Cochrane was obliged to put back into port, and spent some time in dealing with the ringleaders of this mutiny.

Next, when the Chilean Government agreed to make

rockets for him to attack Callao, these failed to explode—
not surprisingly, since the Spanish prisoners who, for
economy's sake, had been ordered to make them, had filled
the rockets with horse manure instead of gunpowder. When,
a week or two later, he tried to use explosion ships against
the heavily defended port, the ships sank before they
reached their objective.

Captains Guys and Spry made the most of these failures.
Even the Chilean people, because they had expected so
much, began to grumble. Cochrane must do something
spectacular, and do it quickly, if his prestige and position
were not to vanish. He decided to try a *coup* which, on the
face of it, was more desperate than any of his previous
exploits. It was nothing more nor less than a direct attack on
Valdivia, a port which commanded the one Chilean province
still in Spanish hands, and which was the base of operations
for Spain's South American fleet. Success there would
finally drive the Spaniards from Chile, and would open at
least the southern coasts to trade. But success looked unlikely.

Valdivia itself lay some distance up a river which ran down
into a beautiful anchorage, protected by great natural
advantages and by every device which the Spaniards could
contrive. The entrance to this anchorage from the sea was
only three-quarters of a mile wide. From each side of it
great cliffs rose up in a semicircle, and on these cliffs forts,
mounting 118 guns, not only commanded the entrance but
also every section of the anchorage itself.

The forts on the eastern cliffs could not be reached from
the sea at all, standing as they did on the edge of a precipice.
It was just possible to reach the forts on the western cliff
from the sea, for a track running from the town linked each
of the forts and then ran down to the shore. But in the last

few hundred yards between the foremost fort and the sea, this track ran steeply down the cliff, and was so narrow that only one man at a time could pass along it. The final stretch, towards the bottom, was so lashed by spray that no one could keep a firm foothold. Throughout its length the track was flanked by dense forest, and though once it had reached the cliff top it widened considerably it was covered between the first and second forts in the chain by three specially placed guns.

So, even if attackers reached the first fort in safety—even if they took that fort, which itself was heavily guarded—they could be stopped by these guns, or at least driven into the forests. Even if they silenced the guns, they would still have to face other forts along the cliff edge.

Yet this was the position that Cochrane decided to attack. Obviously it was a dangerous project, but he did what he could to prevent it from being a rash one. Using the 'resistance' technique he had developed in Spain, he made contact with patriots in the town and province of Valdivia beforehand, and from them he learned not only the layout of the forts and the details of the path which connected them, but also the size and number of such men-of-war which at the moment were lying in the anchorage. Armed with this knowledge, he laid plans to take the forts, town, ships and harbour at one go.

When he was ready, he summoned his officers, and outlined his plans. Even Major Miller, by far the bravest of them all, was aghast.

'Sir,' he said, 'this undertaking is impossible!'

'Major, we must take Valdivia. Sooner than put back it would be better that we all went to the bottom.'

After long discussion and detailed explanations, his

officers began to catch Cochrane's enthusiasm. They agreed that the thing could be done, and the flagship sailed with two smaller ships—the only others that Cochrane was able to man.

They nearly did go to the bottom, and before they were even in sight of Valdivia. In the flagship *O'Higgins*, Cochrane, besides himself, had only two officers and a midshipman. He had to put one of these officers under arrest almost at once for insubordination. The other was incompetent. Cochrane therefore had to act as captain, navigator and officer of the watch. During the voyage he became so worn out through lack of sleep that when the wind dropped and the *O'Higgins* was becalmed he turned in for a rest, leaving the ship in charge of the incompetent lieutenant.

'Wake me at once the moment there's a sign of a breeze.'

No sooner had Cochrane gone below, however, than the lieutenant turned in too, leaving the motionless ship in charge of the midshipman. The midshipman did remain on deck, but fell fast asleep. While he was asleep, a breeze sprang up and carried the *O'Higgins* inshore on to some rocks, which tore off her false keel and caused a serious leak.

As Cochrane scrambled on deck, pulling his clothes on him and wiping the sleep from his eyes, he found that the whole of the ship's company, including the officers, were preparing to abandon ship.

Cochrane exploded the strongest Scottish language he could summon and threw in every Spanish oath he had learned.

'Don't you realize, you swives, that there are only enough boats to take the half of you? What's going to happen to the other half when the boats are gone? Anyway, just look at that surf. See how it's pounding on the rocks. Do you think a boat would live for a second in that?'

The seamen knew that their captain was right. Anyway, they were cowed by his invective. When their first panic had subsided, Cochrane looked round him.

There was already five feet of water in the hold, and those damned pumps were not working.

'Carpenter, get below and clear those pumps!'

The carpenter shuffled below, and when in half an hour there was no sign either of him or of the pumps beginning to work, Cochrane followed him. The carpenter looked at the pumps, shook his head from side to side, and glanced guiltily at his captain.

'My God!' said Cochrane. 'The man doesn't know his job. Here, give me your tools.'

Cochrane dashed up on deck. 'Miller!' he shouted. 'Set every blessed man to bail.' Then, pulling off his coat, he went below again and himself set to work. In two hours the pumps were working again.

'Well, that's that. Now for the leak!'

Rejecting the services of the useless carpenter, he located the leak, and mended that too himself. The ship was seaworthy again. But now there was more bad news. A breathless gunner came running to him.

'The powder magazine's flooded, sir. The ammunition's done for.'

Apart from the small supply on deck and round the waists of the seamen, there was nothing left which the men could fire.

The men looked at their captain. Surely now he would turn back? Cochrane looked back at his men. His ship might spring a fresh leak at any time. He was virtually without ammunition. But he would still go on to attack the position which, at the best of times, many experts considered impregnable.

'We'll go at them with the bayonet. Spaniards don't like steel,' he said.

They sailed on towards Valdivia.

*   *   *

'Now, Miller, this is what I'm going to do. I'm going to pack the flagship off out to sea. I expect the Spaniards are suspicious enough already, without seeing a great frigate coming at them. We'll make do with the two smaller ships. Transfer your marines into them at once.'

The marines under Miller were transferred, and Cochrane with them. The *O'Higgins* turned away to sea.

'Hoist Spanish colours!'

Cochrane would not leave any trick untried. The two smaller ships, with Spanish flags at their mastheads, came slowly inshore, until they were in full view of the anchorage. They then anchored and signalled for a pilot.

The Spaniards were on the alert. They knew well enough that Cochrane was in command of the Chilean Navy. They had learned by now not to take chances.

'Send your boat for the pilot,' they signalled back. They would soon see if these ships were Spanish or not.

Cochrane rubbed his chin. 'Yeoman, tell them we have not got any boats. We are Spaniards just arrived from Cadiz, and all our boats have been washed away rounding Cape Horn.'

The Spaniards too rubbed their chins. They sent neither boat nor pilot. Instead, Cochrane saw a body of fully armed troops, helmets glinting in the sun, scrambling down the path from the foremost fort to this only landing place outside the harbour. Through his telescope he could see that the other forts were standing to.

For a time the soldiers on shore, and Cochrane, with his marines and seamen lying just offshore, stared at each other across the water. Then suddenly all Cochrane's pretences were exposed and Spanish suspicions confirmed to the full. Cochrane had lowered all his boats over the seaward side to hide them from the shore. Now one of them, improperly secured, drifted astern and was seen by the enemy.

So his boats had been washed over coming round Cape Horn, had they? The Spaniards opened fire, and their first shot killed two of Cochrane's men.

Again the Chilenos looked at their captain. They knew he had meant to attack by night, after capturing the pilot and getting the latest information from him. But the Spaniards had seen through his tricks. They had sent no pilot. Worse, they had opened fire at easy range.

'If this goes on we'll all be killed before sundown. Surely we should turn back,' they said.

Cochrane would not turn back. He would not even draw out to sea.

'Miller,' he said, 'we must land at once and drive those men off the beach. Take forty-four marines in the launch and get ashore.'

'Away launch!'

Miller, sitting precariously on an oar placed athwart the gunwales, took the tiller. Then he lowered himself more comfortably to a seat in the stern sheets. As he did so, a bullet went through his hat. Had he been sitting on the oar he would have been killed.

'Always look to your comfort, lads!' he said, taking off his hat.

The launch pulled steadily through surf, whipped up not only by wind but also by bullets. Then, with bayonets fixed and Miller at their head, the landing party leaped ashore and dashed straight for the still-firing Spaniards on the beach. The Spaniards saw the flash of bayonets and their aim faltered. Those crazy men were still coming on! They must be devils indeed! The beach party turned and began scrambling for safety up the narrow path which led to the forts. Miller and his men helped them on their way with one volley from the precious store of ammunition which remained.

The beach was now clear, and Cochrane sent other launches ashore. By nightfall he had landed five hundred men without further opposition. Then he himself took to the gig. He would row under the foot of the western cliff, and from there direct the attack he had planned on the western chain of forts.

The plan worked perfectly. In single file and in absolute silence, Miller's attackers clambered and slithered up the steep path, expecting at any moment to meet a hail of shot from the cliff top. But there were no flashes to pierce the darkness. They reached the top and crawled stealthily towards the first fort. Some distance away from it they halted, except for one tiny detachment. This detachment, under a fat, high-spirited Chilean ensign, Vidal, kept steadily on, under cover, not only of the darkness but also of the thick forest which lined the now broadening path. At last they were almost under the fort itself, and here they too halted.

'Lie down and keep quiet until I come back,' said Vidal. He crept close to the front of the fort. The only entrance there was by ladder up to the top of a wall. The ladder was withdrawn. Vidal squirmed his huge bulk through the trees and round to one flank of the fort. There he crept close again, looking for an obstacle of which he had been warned. He found it. It was a narrow moat. But he also found a fallen tree-trunk which would make some sort of bridge. He slid noiselessly across it and began to feel his way along the side of the fort itself.

The massive wall at the front did not continue all the way round the sides and to the rear. After all, this foremost fort was not likely to be attacked from the rear, where it was protected by the second fort in the chain. The Spaniards had decided that, in the rear, wooden palisades would be protection enough. Vidal pressed the palisades—they were firm. He crept farther along and pressed again. A plank in the palisades gave under the pressure; it was rotten. Through the hole he had made, Vidal could see the inside of the fort itself. He decided to push his way through, but the rotten plank was narrow. He could not squeeze his bulk through it. He swore under his breath. But then, stripping off his greatcoat and tunic, he tried again. There was now just room for him to get through.

As quietly as he had come, he went back through the hole again, across the moat by the fallen tree-trunk, and returned to his party. Then, sending a messenger back to Miller, he led the way through the trees to the palisades and the hole he had made. He and his party were just abreast of this hole when a burst of firing from the front of the fort suddenly woke the night and the defenders in the fort. It was Miller and his men firing off rounds of ammunition as a diversion. At once the fort was alive. All the Spanish defenders rushed to man the wall at the front. Obviously the attack was coming there.

Vidal's party quickened their pace. They crossed the moat, forced their way through the hole in the palisades, and then in their turn began to fire.

Sudden·panic now swept the Spaniards. In the darkness they could see flashes from pistols and muskets in front of them. Now suddenly flashes were coming from the flank, and indeed from inside the fort itself. They were being surrounded. In the dark they could not see what size of force was against them. They did not even try to see. They rushed headlong through the fort and out of the back, and there crashed full tilt into a column of men who had been sent to help them from the fort behind. Fleeing defenders and their would-be helpers got hopelessly mixed up in panicky confusion, and in the meantime the main body of Miller's party burst through Vidal's hole in the palisades and now firing pistols, now brandishing their bayonets, they tore into the struggling mass before them. Defenders and their reinforcements felt the shot and saw the bayonets. They turned and ran for dear life towards the second fort.

Here was the stretch of path covered by the three carefully placed guns. But in the confusion the men who manned these guns could not distinguish friend from foe. They only knew that there was panic and pursuit. They promptly abandoned their guns and joined the panic.

Farther down the path, the men in the second fort heard Spanish cries for help and the sound of running feet. Obviously their comrades in the first fort had been surprised by overwhelming force and were running back for safety. The gates of the second fort were thrown wide open to receive them. But by now the pursuers were on the heels of the pursued. Indeed, the two lots were intermingled. They poured through the gates of the second fort together,

Miller, Vidal and their men bayoneting any Spaniard they caught.

The Spaniards in the second fort caught the terror of their comrades, and with them dashed out of the rear of that fort, along the path which led to the third, their pursuers firing and jabbing at them as they ran. The mob reached the third fort, whose gates were opened to receive them. No one paused for a second. The whole crowd poured through and on down the path to the fourth fort.

And so it went on. The Spaniards fled, scrambling along the path in the darkness, pursued by bayonets through fort after fort, until no forts were left. They then leapt over the cliff, or plunged into the forest. In the course of the night five hundred men had taken eight heavily gunned forts, manned by some two thousand Spaniards. A hundred of the enemy had been killed, a hundred more had been captured, and still many more hundreds had been driven over the cliffs or into the forests.

Cochrane had planned to attack the forts on the eastern cliff in the morning, along the only path, which came from inland. So, at first light, risking their guns, he rejoined the *O'Higgins* and sailed her straight into the harbour. But by now the defenders of these eastern forts could see across the water to where the Chilean flag flew from the eight forts on the western side: and here was a large frigate, with its guns bared, coming in to the attack. The defenders of the eastern forts ran inland for their lives.

Pausing up-river at the town of Valdivia only to do some looting, the fugitives dispersed into the interior. And the Spanish seamen in the small men-of-war which were lying at anchor in the harbour, realizing that the guns of the forts, instead of being a protection, could now be used against them, and seeing the *O'Higgins* sailing majestically towards them, surrendered their ships without a fight. Had they waited only a few minutes, they would have seen this frigate run helplessly ashore. She had sprung a new leak, and Cochrane was compelled deliberately to beach her on a shoal to prevent her from sinking.

He at once set his men to repair her, and himself went up-river to the town. There he found that many of the inhabitants, terrified by the looting of the Spaniards, had rushed into the forests for safety. His first act was to issue a proclamation that neither life nor property would be touched. He then sent some of the remaining inhabitants into the woods with word of this proclamation. By and by the fearful citizens returned to look on their conqueror—or deliverer.

They saw a tall young man, heavy-eyed with sleeplessness, wet and dirty from the night's activities, yet smiling and kindly. They were surprised. They were still more surprised when their deliverer, brushing his mud-stained uniform as best he could, proceeded to give them a short lecture on the elements of democracy. They were, he said, to provide themselves with ballot-boxes. That done, they were to elect a Government from their number who would act as the representative of the Chilean Government in Valparaiso. A little bewildered, but wholly relieved, the inhabitants of Valdivia did as they were told by the young nobleman from Scotland.

As a result of this night's work, the whole province behind Valdivia fell into the hands of the independent Chilean republic, and was never again recaptured by the Spaniards.

News of this astonishing victory reached Valparaiso at a moment when the intrigues of Captains Guys and Spry and the reports of Cochrane's earlier failures had been so effective that Señor Zenteno, the Minister of Marine, was openly calling for Cochrane's impeachment.

Amid the outburst of popular enthusiasm which now followed the latest news, Zenteno was forced to withdraw his proposal and show smiles which he did not feel.

8. Cutting out the 'Esmeralda'

SINCE THE SPANIARDS had now been driven out of the province of Valdivia, Chile's independence was almost complete. But her neighbour, Peru, was still in Spanish hands and a Spanish fleet remained in the Pacific. O'Higgins, the Director of Chile, now agreed that Cochrane and the Chilean fleet should combine with a land force under San Martin to drive the Spaniards out of Peru.

Cochrane produced a number of schemes for winning Peru by combined operations, but San Martin, as the supreme commander, rejected them all, and in fact kept his army immobile for many weeks. The reason for this delay—and for his seeming generosity towards O'Higgins over Chile —became clear later, when, after Cochrane on his own had broken the back of Spanish resistance, San Martin marched into Lima with his intact army and seized power for himself over the fabulously rich country.

Cochrane did not suspect such a trick. But he soon grew restive under the delays, and decided to make an attack, without San Martin's permission or even knowledge, on the port of Callao, where what remained of the Spanish fleet was lying. This fleet consisted of the *Esmeralda*, a forty-four-gun frigate, which itself was larger than the *O'Higgins* and was manned by some of the finest seamen in the Spanish Navy; two other frigates; a corvette; ten smaller ships and twenty-seven gunboats. In all the fleet carried 350 guns. The project seemed almost as impossible as the attack on Valdivia.

As they lay at anchor in the harbour, the Spanish ships were protected by their own guns, by a strong boom which, except for a continuously guarded tiny opening, stretched right across the harbour mouth, and by twenty-eight block-ships. Behind and on either side of the ships there were the 160 guns of the forts which surrounded the harbour. Once again the Spaniards appeared to be in an impregnable position. Yet Cochrane, with only one ship, the *O'Higgins*, and with a force consisting of 160 seamen and eighty marines, decided to attack

He had already reconnoitred the harbour, sometimes at night rowing in his gig and sometimes by day with his telescope as he lay offshore in the *O'Higgins*. As usual, too, he had managed to establish a spy ring of some of the many Peruvians who wanted to be rid of Spain. From his own observations, and the information sent to him by his agents, he already had a complete picture of the harbour. He also learned that there were two frigates, one American and one British, at anchor. He took pains to find out what lights these frigates were showing at night to mark their neutrality.

When he arrived off Callao, he spent three days at anchor instructing his crews in the jobs they were to do. During the afternoon of November 5th, 1820, immediately before the attack was planned to take place, the ships which had accompanied the *O'Higgins* were to weigh anchor and put out to sea as though they had sighted hostile sail and were

139

giving chase. The Spaniards in port had, of course, seen a considerable force arriving offshore. Obviously an attack was planned. But now that almost the whole of this force had put to sea again, clearly the attack would not come that night. So the Spaniards reasoned—just as Cochrane hoped they would. They could relax for another twenty-four hours.

But on the *O'Higgins* there was no relaxation. The 240 volunteers who were to make the attack were dressing in white uniforms with a blue band on the left arm, so that they could recognize each other easily in the dark. They were armed with cutlasses and pistols, split into parties, each with its specific job. The parties stood by the fourteen boats which would soon put off from the *O'Higgins*.

The plan was, first, to capture the flagship *Esmeralda* with the Spanish admiral and his staff on board. The *Esmeralda's* guns were then to be turned on the other frigates, the corvette and the brigs. Under cover of these guns, boarding parties were to take the other men-of-war. Still other parties were to cut adrift the Spanish merchant ships nearest the boom, and two boats' crews were to set fire to two of the block-ships and cut them adrift, to cause flaming havoc among the remaining ships.

There was one last refinement. Having made a flowery address to his Chilean seamen, and told his British and American seamen simply to give the Spaniards a gunpowder plot which they would not forget, he said: 'Chilenos, when you board, do not give your normal battle-cry. Shout instead: "*Viva el Rey!*" The Spaniard may think that we are royalists who have boarded in error. Anyway, it should confuse them!'

The night once again was dark, when at midnight, with oars muffled and in complete silence, the fourteen boats pushed off from the *O'Higgins* and pulled towards the boom. It was so dark that Cochrane's boat, leading the way in, actually collided in the narrow entrance to the boom with the Spanish patrol boat on guard there. That might have ended the attack there and then. But when challenged Cochrane whipped out his pistol and put it to the head of the sentry.

'Keep silent or die!' he said in Spanish. The sentry preferred to keep silent.

Then, as each boat came through the entrance and passed the British frigate lying at anchor there, it was loudly challenged by the British officer of the watch. Cochrane believed that this was done deliberately to give him away. He was bad friends with the captain of this particular frigate. Luckily the challenges were not heard, except by the patrol boat, which was itself now under guard, and when the boats passed the American frigate, which lay farther up the harbour, the American officer of the watch made no challenge. He merely whispered 'Good luck!' as the boats slid by.

As Cochrane had hoped, the *Esmeralda* had been lulled by the afternoon's manœuvre. Her ship's company was asleep below, except for a few sentries. Because of the darkness, the muffled oars and the silence, these sentries did not spot the boats until they were actually alongside. Cochrane's parties boarded at various points simultaneously, and dashed at once to the part of the ship for which they had been detailed. Cochrane himself, boarding by the main chains, was hit by the butt-end of a sentry's musket and fell back into the boat, where the thole-pin drove itself into his body near the spine. The injury was so severe that he felt pain from it for the rest of his life, and in fact finally had to have an operation to relieve it just two years before his death.

None the less he immediately climbed back from the boat to the *Esmeralda* and was promptly shot through the thigh. But he bound a handkerchief tightly round the wound, and carried on not only directing the fight but taking part in it. Indeed, for once he was well supported by Captain Guys. The pair of them stood shoulder to shoulder, slashing with their cutlasses at anyone who came near.

As soon as the sentries gave the alarm the men below tumbled out of their quarters and raced on deck, but in the darkness their sleep-filled eyes could not tell friend from enemy. Nor could they tell how many attackers had actually boarded. For, as Cochrane called in turn to each of his parties, they promptly answered 'Fore top correct, sir,' 'Main top correct, sir,' and so on right through the ship. The bewildered Spaniards heard these shouts coming first from one place, then from another, until it must have seemed that all was already lost. None the less they fought with great bravery, but within a quarter of an hour they were compelled to surrender.

By now the forts were thoroughly awake and were firing indiscriminately. Indeed, a Spanish shot wounded the captain of the *Esmeralda* after he had been taken prisoner. The two neutral ships were also hit, and cut their cables in order to get out of range. Cochrane now made things even more difficult for the forts by hoisting on the *Esmeralda* the neutral lights which were carried by the British and American frigates. Not being able to make head or tail of what was happening, the forts quickly ceased firing.

Unfortunately Cochrane himself was now so weak from loss of blood and from pain that he had to be carried into his boat, and Captain Guys, taking charge in his absence, and contrary to the instructions which Cochrane had given him, cut the *Esmeralda*'s cables and got her under way for the harbour entrance and the open sea. This meant that her guns could not be used as Cochrane had intended, to fire on the other ships. But for this, it is probable that Cochrane would have captured or put out of action every other ship in the harbour. As it was, he had to be content with the capture of only the *Esmeralda*. But this, in fact, proved to be enough.

The cutting out of the *Esmeralda* was on its own one of the most brilliant actions in naval history. Two hundred and forty men in small boats had captured a powerful frigate, manned by 370 of the best seamen and marines that the Spaniards could muster. In the whole action they killed a total of 160 men, captured 200 more, and in addition took the admiral, his staff and all his plans. This was done under the protection of powerfully manned forts and forty other warships.

But the effect of the action was even more striking than its immediate brilliance. Captain Basil Hall, who was then commanding the British ship *Conway* in the Pacific, wrote later that the loss of the *Esmeralda* 'was a death-blow to the Spanish naval force in that quarter of the world; for although there were still two Spanish frigates and some smaller vessels in the Pacific, they never afterwards ventured to show themselves, but left Lord Cochrane undisputed master of the coast'.

The Spaniards on shore at first could not believe that Cochrane had been able to enter the harbour, or that, having done so, he had managed, unaided, to win such an astounding victory. The work must have been done by the American frigate, sheltering under her neutral lights. So when, next morning, this frigate sent a boat ashore for stores, the whole boat's crew was immediately massacred.

What at last it was realized that Cochrane had in fact won the victory himself with such a small force, the shock was felt not only in Callao but throughout Peru. What Cochrane could do to Callao, it was felt, he could do anywhere else. The Spanish garrisons lost heart, and San Martin, deciding that the time was now ripe for his *coup*, marched into Lima, and thence into other Spanish strongholds, virtually without opposition.

San Martin was soon to treat Cochrane and his seamen with the low cunning he had reserved hitherto for his fellow 'patriots'. Despite the most solemn promises, he left the fleet without pay and near to starvation once it had done its job, in the hope of forcing it to desert Chile and join Peru. Cochrane countered with equal cunning by raiding a treasure ship which San Martin had filled for his own use and paying his men out of that. He then returned to Chile.

San Martin did not last long as Peru's dictator. When he was expelled in 1822, almost the first act of the new Peruvian Congress was to pass this resolution:

'The Sovereign Constituent Congress of Peru, in consideration of the services rendered to Peruvian liberty by Lord Cochrane, by whose talent, worth and bravery the Pacific Ocean has been liberated from the insults of enemies, and the standard of liberty has been planted on the shores of the south, HAS RESOLVED, that the supreme Junta on behalf of the nation shall offer to Lord Cochrane, Admiral of the Chilean Squadron, its most expressive sentiments of gratitude for his hazardous exploits.'

This was the least they could have done. Without Cochrane, neither Chile nor Peru would have won their independence from Spain for many years, if at all.

Cochrane no doubt was pleased with the resolution of

thanks. He might have been even better pleased if either the Chilean or Peruvian governments had paid his seamen properly and had honoured their contracts with himself. However, he did manage at last to get about half his pay, which was more than he got from Brazil, the country which he was next to serve.

9. The Chase

WHEN NAPOLEON invaded Portugal in 1808, the Portuguese royal family fled to Brazil, giving this colony a political importance equal to that of the mother country; and in 1821, when Don Pedro VI at last returned to Lisbon, he emphasized this importance by leaving his eldest son Pedro behind as Regent.

Disturbing rumours, however, soon began to reach Lisbon. Brazil, like other South American colonies, was suffering from French Revolution fever. It was said that even the younger Pedro himself was favouring independence. He had better come home at once. But when the recall instructions arrived from the Cortes, Brazilian restiveness burst into flame. The younger Pedro was almost literally besieged by his people.

'You must stay here with us!' they said. When he agreed, the Brazilian people delightedly declared their independence of Portugal and proclaimed young Pedro as their new Emperor.

This was exciting and satisfactory as far as it went. But Brazil's three great northern provinces of Maranhao, Pará

and Bahia were still as strongly held as ever by Portuguese
garrisons. It was no use trying to drive out these garrisons
by land forces, because there were no roads from the south;
and an operation by sea seemed out of the question, since the
Portuguese fleet commanded the whole coastline, with one
ship of seventy-four guns, one of fifty, one of forty-four, one
of twenty-eight, five of twenty-six, two of twenty-two,
one of twenty and one of eight guns. This on paper looked
far more formidable than the Spanish fleets which Cochrane
had virtually destroyed in Chile and Peru. True, the Portuguese who manned these ships were no fighters; but neither
were the seamen who manned the 'independent' Brazilian
fleet; and in numbers the Brazilian ships consisted of one
first-class frigate, the *Pedro Primiero*, sixty-four guns,
another smaller frigate, the *Piranga*, a clipper called the
Maria da Gloria, and five tiny brigs—in no way comparable
to its Portuguese opponent.

None the less the newly formed Brazilian Government
invited Cochrane to command this force, drive the Portuguese
from the seas, and so to free the great northern provinces. As
he had finished his work in Chile and Peru, he agreed; but
he was soon to wish that he had not.

The Brazilian ministers were shifty. So were many of the
seamen. The Brazilian Navy offered its ratings only half the
pay of a Brazilian merchant seaman, with the result that only
the dregs of the waterfronts joined at all; and of those who
did join, some were fifth-column Portuguese royalists.

In Cochrane's first action against the Portuguese, four of
his ships mutinied. Even the *Pedro Primiero* stopped firing
after a few rounds, and when Cochrane rushed down to
investigate he found that the men in charge of the powder
magazine were Portuguese fifth columnists. They had tied

up the 'powder monkeys' who normally carried powder from the magazine to the guns. Naturally the guns could not fire.

Almost worse than the seamen was the state of the majority of the ships. Apart from the *Pedro Primiero* and the *Maria da Gloria*, they were slow sailers; and the *Maria* herself was made of unseasoned wood, which warped and let in the water. The cartridges were more of a menace to the men who fired them than to the targets at which they were fired. The sails fell to pieces in the lightest wind.

Choicest of all, the negro marines refused to help in washing the decks, or even in cleaning their own berths. They had demanded and received personal servants to look after them. Yet these grandees could not handle a sword at all and, with guns in their hands, were more dangerous to friend than to foe.

Cochrane never risked taking the whole of this zoo to sea. Once, with the five least unserviceable ships, manned by the least unruly or incompetent of his seamen, he did put out to meet the whole of the Portuguese fleet. But this, the one and only chance of his career of conducting a fleet action, ended in farce.

Seeing a gap in the enemy's line, he dashed into it with the flagship, and, signalling the other ships to attack four Portuguese who were now separated from the main fleet, he stood ready to hold off all the remaining Portuguese ships on his own. To his fury, however, not one of his four other ships obeyed his order. As usual, they had mutinied. Cochrane could only withdraw from the action—which he did without loss.

After this, there was only one thing to do. He put the whole of his alleged fleet into harbour except the flagship and the *Maria da Gloria*. These he manned with the few good seamen he had, mainly British and American. Then with these two ships he began to blockade Bahia, the port into which the Portuguese fleet had just sailed after the abortive action, and which commanded one of the three occupied provinces.

The blockaded Portuguese fleet was enormously superior in numbers and fighting power, though not in fighting qualities, to Cochrane's two ships. But the blockade was completely successful. Every merchant ship which tried to enter or leave the port was captured. The Portuguese seamen and garrisons and the civilian inhabitants of Bahia soon ran short of food.

'They're hungry, are they?' said Cochrane, when one of his agents brought him news of the discontent inside Bahia. 'Well, let's see if we can't make them frightened as well!'

More than half his fleet was lying idle and useless in Rio de Janeiro. He sent orders to his officers there: 'Set your men on to building explosion vessels. We will blow the Portuguese fleet right out of Bahia. See that the work is done quickly and, above all, secretly.'

Cochrane probably did not expect the work to be done at all. But he could be certain that if he ordered secrecy, his plans would be reported to Bahia at once. He was right. Within a few days everyone in the blockaded port knew that explosion ships were on their way, and the news for the moment checked the boastings even of the Portuguese admiral. He knew, and everyone in Bahia knew, what Cochrane had done in Aix Roads. In Bahia the devastation would be worse; for the anchorage was a small basin seven miles up-river, alongside the town itself. In such a confined space, explosion ships would blow everything to bits.

Cochrane played on these fears. His own fifth column infiltrated into the town and spread rumours. The explosion ships were the largest ever built. They were to be floating earthquakes. What they blew up would never come down. The Portuguese rolled their eyes and soon were wringing their hands. What could they do? Flight into the interior? Cochrane would have them in a trap and blow them prematurely into the next world. They must escape by sea and join their compatriots farther north.

This near-panic was duly reported back to Cochrane as he lay with his two ships off the mouth of the river. The Portuguese admiral, still half full of bombast, could not offer bread, but he could still make speeches.

'Fellow citizens,' he said, 'we will withdraw to Maranhao, where we cannot so easily be blockaded. As you see, we have many merchant ships. There will be room in them, not only for the garrisons, but also for any civilians who want to come with us; and we can carry your valuables too. Have no fears! The whole convoy will be under the protection of my men-of-war. See the size of our fleet! This British admiral with his two small ships—he will not dare to attack us!'

Cochrane read the reports of such speeches with interest. This was just what he wanted. Even if his explosion ships were ever built and ever arrived, it would be an almost impossibly difficult task to tow them seven miles up a winding and, at times, narrow river, which was protected by patrol ships and forts. So long as the Portuguese stayed anchored in Bahia, they would be safe, even though uncomfortable. He must winkle them out. It looked as though he was succeeding. But one never knew with these admiral orators. He had better prod this particular one into action.

Some days later his agents reported that a few nights hence there was to be a grand ball in Bahia. All the naval officers would be attending.

'Ah!' said Cochrane. 'I think that I will attend too.'

His officers probably thought that he intended to row up-river in the gig. In darkness a small boat might slide past the guardships and enter the basin unobserved. Cochrane could then have a good look round and return to his ship.

'To hell with the gig!' said Cochrane. 'I'm taking the flagship!'

El Diablo must be mad after all. Take a big ship at night up a river he had never even seen before? Why, he hadn't even any chart! He'd run on a sandbank for sure! Anyway, how would he get past the guard-ships? And even if he did, he would be trapped in the basin by the whole Portuguese fleet. Truly the idea was madness!

Cochrane did not argue. For once he kept his intentions to himself. He was not going to risk spoiling his effects by having his plans broadcast to the Portuguese.

All afternoon on the day of the ball, the *Pedro* lay well out to sea. Then, towards sundown, she hoisted British colours, and sailed into the river mouth, with her navigation lights burning brightly. In the half light, Cochrane stared intently at the banks, noting every feature. He would have to come back in the dark, and one false move would run him aground. A mile or so up-river he met the first Portuguese patrol ship, and at once answered her challenge.

'We are a British merchantman, bound for Bahia from London. We carry food supplies.'

The *Pedro*'s guns were concealed. It was difficult in the twilight to tell merchantman from warship. Then she was flying British colours, and didn't she say that she was carrying food? Bahia needed all the food she could get. The patrol vessel let her pass.

The *Pedro* nosed on, using the flowing tide and the generally following wind as best she could. The moon was not yet up. The stars were out, but shone no more brightly than the ship's pale navigation lights. Here was a merchantman, exhausted by her buffetings across the Atlantic, and nearing safe harbour at last.

The *Pedro* reached the basin just as the moon rose. The moonlight touched her sails with ghostliness as she slid gently into the heart of the Portuguese fleet. The town itself was ablaze with lights. The sound of music carried across the water to where duty watches and officers of the day grumbled at their luck. To be aboard tonight of all nights! Some watches had all the luck! The Portuguese look-outs stared at the gaily lit town, drank in the nostalgic music reminding them of home, listened to the gentle gurgle of the current against their ships. But—was all that sound just gurgle?

'My God, here's a ship coming in! What on earth! A ship coming up-river at night? If she must do that, why choose this night of all nights?'

'Stand to!'

Seamen left their cards, or tumbled out of their hammocks, cursing freely. Cochrane and the *Pedro* glided on.

'This is no merchantman! It's . . . by God . . . It's that devil in his flagship! Alarm to arms! Inform the admiral!'

The admiral was on shore finding new adjectives to

describe the might of Portugal and, from time to time, dancing.

What were the men he had left behind aboard to do? Here was Cochrane right in their midst. They could fire at him. The skeleton guns' crews were ready. They might even hit him. But in that confined space, already packed with their own ships, they were sure to hit friend as well as enemy.

'Why doesn't the admiral come?'

The admiral was still ashore, raising his glass to the beauty of Bahia. Suddenly, across the room, he saw frantic gesticulations from the door.

'Excuse me, ladies,' he said, and strolled between the dancers to find out what was amiss. A ship had dragged her anchor, no doubt. What a thing to bother him about just now!

A white-faced messenger stood at the door. 'Cochrane and his flagship are in the anchorage, my lord. They are right in amongst us!'

'Impossible!' said the admiral. 'No large ship can come up after dark. Are you drunk?' The admiral refused to leave the ball.

But the messenger persisted. 'This is no ghost, my lord. The Devil himself is here.'

The admiral at least could now see that the messenger was genuinely frightened. Cochrane up here in person? Ridiculous! But something strange *had* happened. With apologies, he called for his cloak and made for the harbour.

Cochrane by now had made certain that the Portuguese knew he was there. It was time to retire. But that damned wind had dropped. He could only get back down-river with the help of the tide. Thank goodness *that* had turned. He let himself drift towards the entrance to the basin, taking a last look round as he went.

'Let go the small anchor. Let her drag. . . . Stand by the capstan to work the cable when I pass the word!'

The Portuguese admiral was just in time to see the *Pedro* disappearing stern foremost down the river, using her anchor both as brake and as rudder.

'The Devil won't get far that way. He'll ground his ship. We'll have him in the morning.'

They did not get the Devil in the morning. The Devil, who had performed the difficult feat of sailing up-river at night, now performed the almost inconceivable feat of drifting down that river, again without chart or sail, and unharmed. He was the Devil indeed.

*   *   *

Next day his agents came aboard from Bahia, bubbling with news. That ghostly visit of the night before seemed to have been the final twang on Portuguese nerves. They were preparing to bolt. But still Cochrane refused to leave anything to chance. He wrote to the admiral, to the general commanding the Portuguese troops, and to the Junta of Bahia, warning them in the name of humanity not to come out, since otherwise they would be set upon by the full might of the Brazilian Navy.

The Portuguese knew the Brazilian Navy. Anyone who could talk about its 'might' must be trying to bluff them into staying where they were, to become helpless victims in an explosion vessel trap. They set sail the following day for the open sea, in a convoy of sixty merchant ships, protected by thirteen men-of-war.

At the mouth of the river, Cochrane waited for them with his two serviceable ships and three brigs which had now joined them.

As usual, he had prepared his plans thoroughly. The ships' companies in his little squadron knew exactly what they were to do. They lay outside the mouth of the river while the vast armada, led by the warships, came stringing slowly downstream. As the Portuguese admiral had forecast, Cochrane made no move. He lay offshore watching. The armada contemptuously sailed past.

Cochrane waited until all the Portuguese ships were clear of the river, the men-of-war in the van and the merchant ships following after. Then he struck at the convoy's rear.

Picking on the sternmost ships as foxes might pick on the last two stragglers from a flock of sheep, the *Pedro* and the *Maria* fired shots across their bows, forcing them to heave to. The Portuguese men-of-war were in the van, almost out of sight. The merchantmen were unarmed. With their sails flapping in the wind, they could only wait, angry and fearful by turns, as their enemies put off boats and closed the narrow strip of water between them.

What would happen to them when these menacing little boats closed the gap completely? Would the Devil take them? Or send them to the bottom of the sea? Or cut their throats?

Cochrane's men climbed on board, but took no notice of the passengers or crew. Instead, some, armed with saws, made straight for the main and mizzen masts, and cut them down, leaving only one tiny sail standing. Others, armed with crowbars, made for the water-casks and stove them in. Still others collected all the ship's arms and ammunition and threw them overboard.

Then their leader spoke to the captain: 'You have now no water, sir; and with that one sail you can only go before the wind. That will take you back to Bahia. Go there at once.'

155

The Portuguese captains could only do as they were told. No Maranhao for them! Only the Bahia they had just left.

Cochrane's boats returned to their ships, and the *Pedro* and the *Maria* set off after the convoy, straggling northwards along the coast. Again they swooped on the last two ships, fired shots across their bows, and forced them to heave to. Again their boats put off, and again their crews cut the main and mizzen masts, stove in the water-casks and threw arms and ammunition overboard.

'Put back to Bahia!'

Cochrane could not afford to put his own men as prize crews on board all these ships. The captures must be forced to sail back on their own. Then the *Pedro* and the *Maria* went off full sail once again after the convoy, and once again swooped on the stragglers.

But by now Bahia was far behind, too far to reach without water and only a single sail. Besides, the next batch of prizes were too valuable to risk on their own. Cochrane signalled the *Maria*: 'Take these into Pernambuco and rejoin when you can.'

The *Pedro* continued the chase on her own, with the little brigs following as best they could far behind.

By the morning of July 4th, two days out of Bahia, the Portuguese admiral was becoming desperate. He was losing ships almost every hour. At this rate he would soon have no convoy left. He must turn and fight, and now was his chance. The *Pedro* was on her own. Thirteen Portuguese men-of-war swung their helms over and turned to tackle the single raider, while the merchantmen and transports made all sail for the north.

Cochrane saw the warships coming, and went about. But

he was still close to the coast. There was not much room for manœuvre. He could easily be hemmed in or driven ashore. He must take care. But the *Pedro* was a magnificent sailer, and Cochrane a magnificent seaman. He tacked this way and that, keeping out of Portuguese range, outwitting his opponents by superior seamanship, drawing the men-of-war farther and farther from the convoy.

This exasperated and alarmed the Portuguese admiral. He was getting nowhere with the elusive Devil. The man just slipped through his fingers. Was this just another of Cochrane's tricks to rob the convoy of its escort and leave it at the mercy of other Brazilian warships which no doubt were lying in wait? The Portuguese admiral gave up his game of tag with Cochrane, and swung round to rejoin his charges. Cochrane followed just in sight until nightfall.

Then he struck again, racing into the middle of the convoy, firing broadsides to right and left. Even those Portuguese who were not paralysed by fear hesitated to fire in case they hit a friend. Cochrane had no such worries. He was alone. Every ship he fired at must be an enemy.

Ship after ship struck her flag. On some Cochrane found as many as two thousand soldiers. He not only, as before, cut the masts, threw overboard the ammunition and stove in the water-casks, but compelled all the officers to give their parole that they would not fight again against Brazil until they had been properly exchanged according to the rules of war. Then he ordered them back to the coast. No one in the *Pedro* slept that night. The Portuguese admiral may have had some rest, but then he was out of harm's way at the head of the convoy.

Through the next morning and into the afternoon, Cochrane continued the chase, swooping, disarming and returning one ship after another to the coast of Brazil. Then, in the late afternoon, he saw that a part of the convoy was changing course. While half a dozen large ships were continuing to sail north towards Maranhao, the men-of-war and all the remainder were turning north-east away from the coast and heading out into the Atlantic.

Cochrane's agents had briefed him well. He knew that the large transports which were continuing on course towards Maranhao were crowded with troops. Obviously they were going to reinforce the garrisons in that province, and so make liberation more difficult. Cochrane decided to follow them instead of the main convoy.

So, leaving the Portuguese admiral in momentary peace, he headed for the largest of the transports, a frigate-built ship. He fired on her until she was brought to. On boarding, he found a division of several thousand soldiers, all fully armed, but impotent under the *Pedro*'s guns. As before, the main and mizzen masts were cut, arms, water and ammunition were thrown overboard, and parole taken from the officers. As an additional prize, Cochrane seized all the regimental flags as a present for the independent people of Brazil. He then went on to attack and stop the five other transports, and just as he had finished his work with them one of his small brigs came into sight. Under the menace of the tiny guns of this brig, Cochrane sent back the six large transports laden with troops to Pernambuco for internment.

It was now high time to get after the admiral and the rest of the convoy. But they were, of course, out of sight, and a haze spreading over the sea made the search more difficult. Had they escaped? Cochrane sat down in his cabin and began to think.

'It looks to me,' he said to his officers, 'as though the

admiral has given up any idea of making Maranhao. Otherwise he would have stuck by his transports. But he sailed off north-east. Can he be making for the Azores? Or even for Lisbon? By God, that's it! I believe the man has turned tail for home.'

Cochrane set course for the Azores. But for five whole days he sailed on steadily and saw nothing. Had he been wrong after all? Perhaps the Portuguese admiral had again altered course in the haze, and was even now delivering bombastic speeches in the port of Maranhao.

Then, on the 11th, there was a shout from the crow's-nest. First, 'Ship in sight dead ahead!', then, 'Three ships dead ahead!', then, 'Convoy in sight dead ahead!'

The men in the *Pedro* came alive again. They had caught the enemy after all. Now the fun would begin all over again. Rapidly they approached their quarry. But then the wind dropped.

For hour after hour the Portuguese convoy and their lone Brazilian pursuer lay becalmed in full view of each other. This was more than the Portuguese could bear. They had sailed out of Bahia inflated with confidence which their admiral had blown into them. But, almost at once, their confidence had been wrecked. One by one, their ships had been picked off, and no one knew what had happened to them. All they had known was that their turn would come soon, if not next. They had raced on to the north, but all the time their heads were turned fearfully over their shoulders, waiting for the raider to pounce. Then, all at once, as by the grace of God, they seemed to have escaped the danger. That devil had gone after the transports and left them alone, and this merciful haze had come out of the sea to protect them. For five days all had been quiet as they headed for home and safety. They relaxed, they began to smile again, and talked to each other of the delights of Lisbon. Then the haze had cleared, and there was the Devil right on their tail, becalmed for the moment it was true, but ready to pounce once again with the first touch of a breeze. They would never see Lisbon now. They could only wait for the worst.

For three whole nights and days they drifted aimlessly in the Atlantic, sleepless and nerve-racked, waiting for the end. Even the oratory of the Portuguese admiral was stilled.

Then, on the 14th, a wind sprang up. Fleeing convoy and pursuing raider together crossed the Equator; but Cochrane was coming up fast. As soon as he was in striking distance, he went straight in for the attack, but, finding that at long last the convoy had learned prudence and was now keeping close together, he hauled off again, waiting until they should separate. So they went on throughout the 15th, the convoy keeping close together, and making no effort itself to attack the raider; the raider waiting in his turn for a chance to pounce.

But Cochrane grew tired of waiting. At 3 a.m. on the 16th, he crowded on all sail and made a dash into the convoy, firing a broadside at almost point-blank range into the side of a frigate and disabling it. Then, just as he was tacking for the kill, there was a rending, tearing noise. His mainsail had split in two and the *Pedro* was stopped almost dead. On the Portuguese decks men went down on their knees as they saw their scourge heave to, and watched the ever-widening gap of water grow between them.

Cochrane set his men at once to repair the mainsail. But he had now to make a decision. As soon as the repairs were done he could resume the chase, harrying and destroying the convoy right across the Atlantic. But his own stores were beginning to run low. He might not be able to replenish them on the other side. Worse, he was thinking of his single little brig, driving those six great transports back to Pernambuco. It would not surprise him if, in the night, some of those transports had broken away from their escort and perhaps made Maranhao. That would never do. His job was to free the province. Clearly, since nothing now would stop the convoy in its headlong bolt for home, he must go back.

Just at that moment the decision was made even more easy; for the *Maria da Gloria*, after seeing her prizes safely into Pernambuco, had put out to sea again, and, coming up with the brig and her transports, had learned that Cochrane had set course for the Azores. She followed, and now came up with the *Pedro*. Cochrane, turning for Brazil himself, ordered the *Maria*, with her stores and ammunition replenished at Pernambuco, to go on after the convoy. So, once again, the unhappy Portuguese, having believed for a second time that they had escaped at last, for a second time suddenly found themselves beset by one of Cochrane's ships.

The *Maria* followed the convoy right across the Atlantic, harrying it as it went, and actually drove into the mouth of the Tagus, and there set fire to four of the merchantmen right under the guns of a Portuguese line-of-battle ship. Then she turned round for home.

Cochrane's chase had lasted from July 2nd until July 16th. It had begun in 13° S.; it had finished near the Canaries in 5° N. In the course of it, some sixty ships—transports, merchantmen and men-of-war—were so disabled that they had to be abandoned, or were forced to return to Brazil. Out of that armada of seventy-three ships which had emerged so confidently from the river mouth at Bahia only thirteen ever reached Lisbon.

By this operation, which a military historian has called 'a feat without parallel in the history of war', Cochrane removed for all time the threat of a Portuguese fleet from Brazil; and in the process he lost neither a single ship nor a single man.

10. Conquest by Bluff

ALMOST ON HIS OWN, without the authority of the Government he served—but to their enormous benefit—Cochrane had captured the port of Bahia and the great province which lay behind it, and he had driven what remained of the Portuguese fleet for ever from the South Atlantic.

Now, speeding back from the chase of the shattered convoy, he set himself to his one last task for the Emperor of Brazil. Bahia was free, but Maranhao and Pará were still in Portuguese hands. Now that their command of the sea was gone, the Portuguese could no longer reinforce their garrisons there. But equally, the Brazilians, except with the aid of Cochrane and the small fleet he commanded, could not hope to dislodge the Portuguese, and so secure the whole of their country by land as well as by sea.

Cochrane was certain that he could free these last two provinces on his own. He believed that he could free them without firing a shot. Anyway, he intended to try. In fact, luck was against him. He did eventually have to fire one shot. But that was only an incident in a bluff which even today is hardly credible.

The bluff began when, on one of the troopships he cut out from the convoy, he found a message. A Portuguese frigate was on its way from Lisbon, and was expected to arrive at Maranhao within the next week. This was just the information he needed.

'So they're expecting a frigate, are they? Well, the *Pedro* is a frigate. They can expect *her*. All we need is a Portuguese flag. Yeoman!'

But the yeoman was already on his way to his locker. As the *Pedro*, that superb frigate, came in sight of Maranhao, she was flying Portuguese colours.

The commandant of Maranhao was jittery. Weeks before he had received definite word from Bahia. All the troops there were coming up to join him. So was the Portuguese fleet. So was an unnamed frigate from Lisbon. With such reinforcements against him, that devil Cochrane could do his worst. Would he try to blockade? This was no Bahia into which a fleet could be cooped to become a sitting target for explosion vessels. This was a wide anchorage, with all the room in the world for manœuvre. If Cochrane tried his tricks he would be hemmed in himself. And if he tried to storm? What could a few seamen do against the present garrisons and the troops which were coming to reinforce them?

The commandant watched the horizon with complacency. Some days later his complacency seemed to be gratified.

'The reinforcements are arriving, my lord,' said a messenger.

The commandant put his telescope to his eye and there, sure enough, two transports, oddly rigged it is true, but unmistakably Portuguese, were moving over the horizon towards the harbour.

'No doubt the rest are following, with the fleet astern of

them to watch out for any mischief Cochrane may try,' he said.

The transports limped over the bar, sailed up the harbour, and made fast. The commandant, slightly puzzled, went down to greet them. At once he became thoroughly alarmed. He heard how the convoy had been attacked, how the transports themselves had been boarded and mutilated, how they had been sent back under strong escort to the coast of Brazil, how—only by skill and supreme daring—they had managed to escape their escort. No doubt the transports omitted to mention that this escort consisted of only a single brig. Perhaps they told the commandant of a line-of-battle ship, or at least of a squadron of frigates which they had eluded.

One certain piece of news they did give—that the remainder of the convoy, accompanied by the whole of the Portuguese fleet, was now heading for Lisbon instead of Maranhao, and was being hotly pursued by Cochrane.

Well, even if that meant no fleet and no further military reinforcements, it at least also meant that for a time there would be no Cochrane.

The commandant resumed his study of the horizon. That frigate from Portugal should soon be here. The quicker the better. Cochrane would have to give up the chase soon, and when he had revictualled at Rio, he would be sure to make for Maranhao.

'Come on, that frigate!'

'That frigate' came on.

There she was at last, just off the bar, signalling for a pilot.

'Captain Garçao, put off at once. No, wait . . . I will send a message to my colleague the captain. . . . Here, take this. . . . Tell him how welcome he is. . . . And warn him that Cochrane will be here soon.'

Captain Garçao put off in a gig, bearing the commandant's messages and congratulations on safe arrival from Lisbon. He drew alongside 'that frigate', climbed the rope ladder which was obligingly dropped for him, stepped on to the quarterdeck, saluted smartly—and was promptly arrested.

'That frigate' was, of course, the *Pedro*.

*   *   *

Cochrane smiled pleasantly at his new prisoner. He took him below, offered him wine, made sure that his gig's crew were comfortable too.

'So you are El Diablo,' said Captain Garçao. 'We have heard much of you; but I have news for you too. You thought you had disabled our transports from Bahia. You did not know that some of them escaped and reached us, did you?'

Cochrane did not know that, though he had feared it. He sipped his wine. 'Oh dear!' he said. 'I thought that the escort I sent with them was strong enough to hold them. Let's see— the escort was five frigates, wasn't it, Lieutenant Grenfell? Did I put five or six frigates in charge of those transports?'

'Only five, my lord. You took the sixth with you in the squadron which was chasing the convoy.'

'Ah yes, of course.'

Cochrane turned to Garçao: 'You are a seaman. You know how it is. With so large a fleet one loses count of all one's ships. Still, even if it was only five frigates, your transports did well to escape. You Portuguese know how to fight. Some more wine, captain?'

'Thank you. We do know how to fight; and I must warn you, sir, that we are preparing to fight even harder in defence of Maranhao.'

Cochrane put down his glass. His smile vanished. 'Captain,'

he said gravely, 'I trust you will do no such thing. I know you are brave, but I hope that you are not rash. You know that our fleet has already routed your great convoy and driven your men-of-war from the coasts of Brazil. Our fleet has returned from the chase. It has replenished its stores and ammunition. Even now it awaits my signal just beyond the horizon. This small ship in which I now have the pleasure of entertaining you'—here Cochrane waved his arm vaguely at the *Pedro*—'is only a single advance unit, and not a very good one, I regret to say. Some more wine? No? Well, perhaps you will allow me the pleasure of showing you round the ship, though I must apologize for its poor state. Please remember, captain, that we have been continuously fighting at sea, and have but now returned.'

Cochrane conducted his visitor round the *Pedro*. Captain Garçao was a first-class seaman. He saw that the ship was in a high state of preparedness, and that she was obviously a first-class man-of-war. If El Diablo called this poor, what must his other ships be like? Captain Garçao stared reflectively towards the horizon, and seemed in the haze to see masts towering away in the distance.

'Captain, I will not deceive you,' said Cochrane. 'The Emperor of Brazil does not pay my seamen as regularly as he should. There has been some discontent. But, happily for us, the convoy which your gallant admiral was escorting contained rich prizes. My fleet has shared in these. The men are now fully content. Further—and you as a seaman will know the truth of this—since their great victory over the armada they are in the highest spirits. It's as much as I can do to contain them. That is why I have left them some miles offshore. The mere sight of your rich town before them might fire them to excess.'

The gallant captain did not doubt the evidence of his own eyes. The *Pedro* certainly was a fine and powerful ship. Now he was trying, not very successfully, to doubt the promptings of his own imagination. There was no sign of any fleet in the offing, but undoubtedly that vast armada had been routed—the evidence of the transports proved that. Were the stories of the fugitives highly coloured? Maybe. But, making all allowances, Cochrane could not have caused such havoc without a formidable force.

Now Cochrane was speaking to him again. 'Captain, I have a proposal to make. You are free to leave the ship as you will. But pray, when you go ashore, tell the commandant that it would be folly to resist. I am a humanitarian. I have no heart for needless slaughter. Beg him to surrender the town. My terms, I assure you, will be most generous. As proof that I wish to avoid bloodshed, I will not summon my fleet until I have word from you. Allow me, please, to give you letters to your commandant and other notabilities.'

Garçao saw in this yet another gesture of a man supremely confident in the force which he commanded. He went ashore wide-eyed, and repeated with Portuguese exaggeration all that Cochrane had told him. He also handed over the letters.

To the commandant of the garrison, Cochrane casually referred to his rout of the Portuguese naval and military forces in Bahia, and declared that he now intended to free the province of Maranhao from foreign domination.

'The naval and military forces under my command,' he wrote, 'leave me no room to doubt the success of the enterprise.' The military forces under his command were nil, and the naval forces consisted of one ship. He went on: 'I am anxious not to let loose the imperial troops of Brazil upon Maranhao, exasperated as they are at the injuries and cruelties exercised towards themselves and their country-men, as well as by the plunder of the people and the churches of Brazil. It is for you to decide whether the inhabitants of these countries shall be further exasperated by resistance which appears to me unavailing.'

To the provincial junta he wrote that he proposed to offer the beautiful province of Maranhao whatever aid and pro-tection they needed against the foreign yoke. He desired 'to hail them as brethren and friends'. If, however, anyone, from self-interested motives, intended to oppose the deliver-ance of their country, the naval and military forces which had driven the Portuguese from the south were again ready to draw the sword in the like just cause. 'The result,' Cochrane concluded, 'cannot be long doubtful. The chief authorities are hereby invited to make known to me their decision, in order that the responsibility of consequences—in case of opposition—may not be imputed to any undue haste in the execution of the duty which I shall have to perform.'

The disclaimer of undue haste in this second letter 'To the Illustrious and Excellent the Provincial Junta of Maran-hao' was especially choice, for haste was exactly what Cochrane needed. At any moment the Portuguese might discover that instead of the large force which was supposed to be ranged against them there was only a single ship. Once they had learned that, even they would be unlikely to give in without a fight.

However, all he could do for the moment was to wait for replies to his letters. The replies were not entirely satis-factory. They did contain offers of surrender, but the sur-render was subject to conditions which Cochrane would not accept. He decided to exert a little pressure. Weighing anchor, he brought the *Pedro Primiero* right through the harbour and into the river leading to the town, a river which never before had been navigated by so large a ship.

The sight of the *Pedro* so close to their town impressed the peering inhabitants. The fact that Cochrane chose to moor her immediately under the guns of well-manned forts convinced them that he had no fear of being attacked himself because of the presumably overwhelming forces which lay at call not far away.

Cochrane spent an impatient night, keeping the ship's company alert in case of a surprise attack, and no doubt planning further moves unless he heard from the shore in the morning. The further moves were not necessary, for on the next day members of the junta, accompanied by their bishop, came aboard, promised unconditional allegiance to Don Pedro, and thereafter agreed to surrender the city, the forts and the garrisons to Cochrane personally. Cochrane sighed with inward relief. But he did not yet know how far, even for the moment, the junta or the bishop could speak for the troops. There was still the serious danger that some individual commander, perhaps of one of the forts which at this moment dominated the *Pedro*, would decide to call Cochrane's bluff on his own responsibility, or that by some means or another word might reach the junta that Cochrane had no force behind him. Despite the official capitulation, Cochrane would then be unable to take the port, and would risk annihilation himself.

He kept his men constantly on watch, and, sure enough, from the deck of his ship, he saw that some of the forts were not pulling down their colours, despite instructions from the junta, and even that some parties of troops appeared to be forming up on the beaches. He had to put a stop to this at once. He fired a shot, harmless but full of threatening intent, right over the town. At once a flag of truce was run up on shore, and Cochrane landed a party under Lieutenant Grenfell to lower the Portuguese flag and hoist Brazilian colours in its place.

But the job was not half finished. Large numbers of Portuguese troops, fully armed, were still in the town, and time was passing. Even the least imaginative or most cowardly of them would soon begin to ask why there was still no sign of that 'overwhelming force'. As soon as the surrender was confirmed they would expect Cochrane to summon his ships from over the horizon and bring them into port. Why did he not do so?

Cochrane sensed all this but went brazenly on. To calm any fears in the civilian population, and as far as possible to bring dissidents over to his side, he issued a proclamation to the people. He was delighted, he said, that their tranquillity and prosperity had not been upset by hostilities. He suggested that all citizens, whether they were Portuguese or not, should be given an opportunity to take an oath of allegiance to the Emperor, and to elect their own provisional government. He did add a sentence or two that if, while the oaths were being taken and the elections were being prepared, anyone tried to disturb the peace, he would know what to expect. But the general tenor of his message was warm and friendly.

His message to the commandant of the Portuguese garrison was equally friendly. He offered the garrison the choice, once they had laid down their arms, either of staying where they were or of taking transport to Portugal or to any other country they cared to choose. And with the courtesy which a Latin would expect, and which came naturally to Cochrane, he ended: 'I have to express my regret at your indisposition, which has deprived me of the pleasure of seeing you. But if circumstances permit I shall avail myself of an early opportunity of paying you my personal respects.' The general-at-arms could make what he liked of this last paragraph.

The declaration of independence of the province from Portugal went off amid great acclamation, and so did the taking of the oath of allegiance to the Brazilian Empire. Many Portuguese who must at first have wanted to flee now decided to remain, and it subsequently became one of Cochrane's duties to protect these people, to whom he had given his word, from the rapacity and vengeance of their Brazilian neighbours.

But though the political side of the *coup* was going well, the fact remained that large numbers of armed Portuguese troops were still in the town and the forts.

Cochrane as quickly as possible collected together from the ships which he found in the harbour sufficient transports for those soldiers who did not wish to remain. Then he courteously but firmly directed the general-at-arms to send all such troops, without arms, to a particular point ready for embarkation.

Unfortunately this operation took up some time, and when it was no more than half complete some of the soldiers still on shore at last began to suspect that Cochrane after all was bluffing. They refused to embark or to lay down their arms. But Cochrane now had a slightly stronger hand to play. Some of the soldiers had already embarked. The ships which they had boarded had been placed under the *Pedro Primiero*'s guns. At any moment Cochrane could have destroyed the lot. 'Tell these men to embark at once or their companions will be destroyed,' he told the general-at-arms. 'My stipulation of safe conveyance to Europe will then be rendered unnecessary.'

This threat, at least, was no bluff. The remaining troops ashore threw down their arms and went on board like lambs.

As soon as they were safely stowed away, Cochrane sent a party of seamen ashore to disarm the local militia. Then, for three whole weeks, almost the complete Portuguese garrison, which could so easily not only have defended the town but have destroyed Cochrane, were forced to sweat it out in their own ships under the guns not only of Cochrane's flagship but also of the Portuguese men-of-war in the harbour, which now were manned by parties from the *Pedro*. By now they knew that they had been bluffed, for as day followed day no more Brazilian ships and no Brazilian troop transports appeared. But there was nothing they could do. They were without arms and were watched continually. At the slightest sign of trouble they knew that they and the boats they were in would be sent to the bottom.

Cochrane was now free to turn his attention once more to the political side of his exploit. He was dissatisfied with the provisional junta which had been elected. These men seemed more concerned with shooting anyone to whom they happened to owe money than with good government. Cochrane lectured them on the virtues of honesty—of which he could hardly claim to have been an exponent during the past few days—and of the sort of democratic government to which people in Britain were slowly becoming accustomed, but which must have seemed wildly strange, not only to illiterate Indians, but also to people who had been educated in South American political habits.

About the only thing, however, which his pupils produced to please him was an extravagant letter of congratulation to the Emperor from the newly elected Maranhao Government. The letter referred to the 'wisdom, prudence and gentle manners of Lord Cochrane which have contributed still more to the happy issue of our political difficulties than even the fear of his force. To anchor in our port—to proclaim independence—to administer the oaths of obedience to Your Majesty—to suspend hostilities throughout the province— to provide proper government—to bring the troops of the country into the town, but only in sufficient numbers to ensure order and tranquillity—to open the communication between the interior and the capital—to provide it with necessaries—and to restore navigation and commerce to their pristine state—all this, Sire, was the work of a few days. Grant heaven that this noble chief may end the glorious career of his political and military labours with the like felicity and success, and that Your Imperial Majesty, being so well served, nothing more may be necessary to immortalize that admirable commander not only in the annals of Brazil but in those of the whole world.'

Some of the hopes expressed in this letter were unnecessary, or at any rate were left miserably unfulfilled, and the language was exaggerated. But the facts it contained were exact.

Cochrane, however, even now was not satisfied. He had secured two vast provinces for Brazil, but a third, Pará, still remained under Portuguese control. He decided to secure that too and by the same trick which had been so successful at Maranhao.

First he sent agents to Pará to spread news both of the dispersal of the Portuguese fleet and of the capitulation of Maranhao. They were also to expatiate on the size of Cochrane's force. Then he told Lieutenant Grenfell to take over the Portuguese brig in which the unfortunate Captain Garçao had first come out to welcome the *Pedro Primiero*, and to proceed in it to Pará, carrying orders written in Portuguese by Cochrane. These orders made it appear that Lieutenant Grenfell and his brig were simply the advance party sent on ahead to see whether, in view of the overwhelming force which was following, they could not secure the port of Pará and the province it commanded, without resort to violence. To make these orders seem more realistic, the date on them was left blank. Lieutenant Grenfell simply filled in the date on which he actually crossed the bar into Pará. The Portuguese commandant and junta would then assume that the orders had been handed over by Cochrane himself on that day, and that he, with his fleets and transports, was lying just beyond the bar.

Grenfell sailed into Pará under a flag of truce and showed these orders to the Portuguese junta, who, thanks to the facts and rumours spread by agents, were already preparing to find El Diablo under their beds. With the exception of the Portuguese commandant, who was shouted down, the inhabitants of the town agreed to switch their allegiance from Portugal to the Brazilian Empire.

So one small brig, manned by a hundred men, secured for Brazil a province which was larger than England and France combined, without losing one man. The only casualty was Lieutenant Grenfell himself. When the Portuguese authorities discovered that he and his brig were on their own, and that there was no vast supporting fleet behind them, they hired a man to murder him. Even this was not successful, for Grenfell got away with a severe wound, and, of course, by this time all the Portuguese troops were disarmed, the guns in their forts were spiked, and they could be dominated by a single brig.

Despite his extraordinary military triumphs, the remainder

of Cochrane's stay in Brazil was not happy. The Brazilian authorities refused to listen to his lectures on the virtues of Adam Smith and John Stuart Mill. They were determined to run their country for the benefit not of the whole people but of themselves alone. Further, they had refused to pay Cochrane's seamen the wages and bounties they had promised, and although they conferred on Cochrane himself the title of Baron of Maranhao they refused to pay him his salary.

By his efforts alone he had secured for them three great provinces. More than that, by destroying or dispersing the Portuguese fleet, he had opened up their coasts to the sea trade which, because of the absence of inland communications, was so essential to living, and he had made certain that their independence would not again be threatened from the Old World. But for these services he did not receive one penny.

He left the country in disgust and returned at last to his native Scotland. But there was to be no rest. Within a year he had plunged into the difficult task of freeing the Greeks from the Turks and the impossible task of freeing the Greeks from themselves. For years he fought his own battles, until one by one all his honours were restored and he was allowed to command a British fleet. At the age of seventy-nine he was still demanding a command in the Crimean War and produced secret war plans which, he claimed, would end hostilities in a week, which were rejected at the time but which were seriously considered and partially adopted fifty years after his death by Mr. Winston Churchill in the first world war.

Right to the end of his life he campaigned to force Admiralty into replacing sail by steam. He devised his own marine engines and boilers, invented new types of propellers, propounded entirely new ideas for the streamlining of ships, pouring out his money, his energy and his inventiveness until Admiralty gave way; and when he died in 1860 at the age of eighty-five he was buried in Westminster Abbey, honoured at last by all the countries, including his own, which he had tried to serve.

But, for the moment, we leave him in Edinburgh, where, after years of absence which had begun under a cloud of disgrace, he and his wife went one night to the theatre, and in their honour the playwright inserted a few lines of reference to South America. As soon as they heard these lines, the whole audience rose in their seats and began to cheer Lord and Lady Cochrane, and as they did so, the colour drained from Lady Cochrane's face. Through all the tempestuousness of his public career, she had given her husband a private serenity. Her love for this boyish genius had been the one certain thing in his life. Both dishonour and glory had surged round her. She had known the fears of personal danger, and the worse fears of the dangers she imagined for her husband when he was at sea. She had known the exhilarations of success and the exasperations of failure. She had faced them all, and would face them all again. But here at this moment was something she could not face unmoved. The play had stopped in mid-act. The players had come to the front of the stage to join with the glittering audience. The clapping grew in intensity, and behind it, low at first, but steadily swelling to a roar, came the sound of voices pouring out their affection and pride. Her husband was home, home at last among his own people, and welcomed by them. Perhaps at that moment a hope flashed through her mind that the days of battling and danger were gone, that now he could be at peace. She would know that the hope was vain, that nothing would change the erratic, brilliant and lovable man she knew, that until he died he would go on living as he had always lived. Yet the thought held her. The tumults, the defeats, the unbelievable triumphs had led to this great moment. The voices of his own people, led by Sir Walter Scott, were now raising him to the stars. Could he not at last be content? Perhaps the sense that Cochrane could never be content, that the peak on which he now stood was just an incident in his life, that his future would be as stormy, as restless and as intense as his past, flooded into her mind, and there mingled with pride and joy in one moment of unbearable emotion. As the ovation reached its climax, Lady Cochrane suddenly caught her husband's arm, and, for the only time in her life, she burst into tears.

Bibliography

Autobiography of a Seaman   DUNDONALD
Dundonald   J. W. FORTESCUE
Life of a Seaman   E. G. TWITCHETT
Lord Cochrane   CHRISTOPHER LLOYD

are the most readable of the books from which I have drawn material for this study of Cochrane's career at sea. I am completing my own work in a second book, *The Worm Had Friends*, which is to be published next spring, and which deals with Cochrane's long fight, in Parliament and out, against conservatism and corruption.